NEXT
GENERATION
FOOTBALL
TRAINING

NEXT GENERATION FOOTBALL TRAINING

OFF-SEASON WORKOUTS USED BY TODAY'S NFL STARS
**TO BUILD PRO ATHLETE STRENGTH AND GIVE YOUR TEAM
THE COMPETITIVE EDGE**

ABDUL FOSTER

Professional Trainer and Fitness Coach, Owner of Nine Innovations Training Facility

PAGE STREET
PUBLISHING CO.

PAGE STREET
PUBLISHING CO.

First published in 2017 by
Page Street Publishing Co.
27 Congress Street, Suite 105
Salem, MA 01970
www.pagestreetpublishing.com

Distributed by Macmillan, sales in Canada by The Canadian Manda Group.

20   19   18   17   1   2   3   4

ISBN-13: 978-1-62414-240-6
ISBN-10: 1-62414-240-0

Library of Congress Control Number: 2016949119

Cover and book design by Page Street Publishing Co.
Photography by Steve Sangalang except pages 30, 54, 74, 98, 122, 148, 174, 198, 224, and 246 by Getty Images.
Written with Kara Yorio

Printed and bound in the United States

Page Street is proud to be a member of 1% for the Planet. Members donate one percent of their sales to one or more of the over 1,500 environmental and sustainability charities across the globe who participate in this program.

This book is dedicated to all of my family, my brothers and close friends who have helped me along the way. Foreverwerun!

CONTENTS

INTRODUCTION: A NEW BREED

At Nine Innovations, my Houston training facility, our tagline is *New Breed*—a new breed of trainer for a new breed of athlete. It's about the muscle, the music, the attitude and mostly the hard work and carefully designed workout, the specific, full-body, intense workout that makes a talented athlete great.

I became a trainer to help mold athletes, and that gave me an opportunity to help my brother, Arian, make the most of his career, pay his bills and provide for his family. For some, working out is a way to be healthier, and that is a great target. For others, for our core clients, it's a livelihood, and I take preparing them for that as seriously as they take their careers.

But I am not just a football star's brother who helped him elevate his career. I was an athlete myself. I competed in the 110-meter hurdles at Florida A&M University and have always had a deep interest in athletic performance.

I received my personal training certification in 2009 and started training Arian immediately after his rookie season. I opened my gym in the spring of 2014. My program is an evolution of what I learned from my certification and education, and it is combined with what I have learned from other trainers and mostly what I have learned from the athletes themselves, particularly football players. We know what players need for success and where their past workouts have failed them. We ask athletes to put their faith in us, and we work very hard to reward their trust.

The three-month Nine Innovations workout that you are about to begin was created to get the most out of athletes, to push them to be their best and to give our clients—who we consider family as much as we do my brother—their greatest chance for success.

THE NINE INNOVATIONS WORKOUT

The Nine Innovations model is the culmination of my years as an athlete, as well as working with my brother, Arian, (and others) so he could achieve his NFL dreams. It is an informed combination of exercises, techniques and specifics I've learned while getting my personal training certification, during my time in school, working with other trainers and during years of helping clients get the most out of their bodies. It has been refined over time through research and in-the-gym experience.

This is a high-intensity training program that caters to your specific needs as a football player. You're going to get stronger. You're going to get bigger. You're going to gain some explosiveness. You can't be great on the field by just being in shape and training hard; you must be in football shape and train specifically for the skills you will need on the field.

At Nine Innovations, we pride ourselves on personalizing workouts for our clients. We watch film footage to see how they play, how they cut or block or run their routes, where they have weaknesses and where their strengths are. We change their program based on our observations and expertise not only before we start training them, but sometimes day-to-day as we go along as well.

But not everybody can get to us in Houston, and I realized this workout could be generalized to benefit all football players, to take a talented young guy with a dream of making it to the NFL and help him make that happen.

My program combines conditioning and strength training, movement and correctives. It is a full-body workout every day even when you're focusing on different parts of the body during strength building. If you follow the plan, not only will you get into great shape overall and become stronger, you will also be quicker on the field. Not only will you become faster at getting from point A to point B, but you will also gain speed endurance, which is the ability to maintain speed over a period of time. This is especially key for guys in skill positions such as running backs.

Each day's workout is broken up into sections. There is nothing arbitrary. Every stretch and every exercise has a specific purpose.

Pay attention to the form noted in the step-by-step instructions. Just doing the exercise isn't enough; to be effective, it must be done right. If you have bad form, not only are you going to fail to meet the goal of that exercise, but you are likely to injure yourself or compensate with the wrong muscle, throwing your body off balance.

Every day will start with the same set of warm-up and movement exercises in the morning followed by a few "correctives," which help correct imbalances that can trigger ailments like hamstring tightness, for example. You cannot just jump into the most difficult, most intense part of the workout. You must warm up to activate the muscles you are going to be using in that day's workout.

The rest of the day is the strength portion of the workout, which is broken into three clusters. The cluster system allows me to control the conditioning and the tempo of the workout, and it allows you to get a total body workout outside of isolating specific muscles. It gives you the freedom to tailor your workout specifically for you as an athlete, specifically for the football player and his needs. You will run through the circuit of each cluster, or block, doing each exercise once for as many repetitions or amount of time as required, and then going back and doing as many circuits as required. The workouts will get more difficult as the weeks go on.

We will eventually add what we call the metabolic workout to the routine. It comes at the end of the day and is intended to get out of you what you didn't think you had left, for you to raise your heart rate one last time and finish the day completely spent.

On Wednesdays, you will have a recovery day from the strength portion of the workout. You will still do the warm-up and movement exercises, but you won't do the strength training. When you're training, you're basically beating up your body Monday, Tuesday, Thursday and Friday. A huge part of getting stronger and getting faster is recovery. When you break down your muscles, they have to rebuild in order for them to get bigger and stronger faster.

It is important to listen to your body. If there is a certain area that doesn't feel 100 percent, wait. Never work out unless you feel you can. Most injuries happen because of fatigue, so be sure to monitor your body, warm up properly and rest on recovery days.

Proper nutrition is also very important. Avoid unhealthy foods while training. Keeping hydrated while working out is also a major factor—drink plenty of water before, during and after workouts.

Each daily workout should take no longer than two hours. Once the routine is somewhat familiar, it should take no longer than an hour and a half.

If something comes up and you can't do a workout one day, do it the next day. Use Wednesday or the weekend as your catch-up period to get back in sync with the weekly schedule. For example, if you miss Thursday's workout, do it on Friday, and do Friday's workout on Saturday. Then pick up with Monday's workout as usual.

We are committed to making you the best player you can be. If you follow this workout, when you take the field you will know you've worked harder and smarter than the guy across from you. You will know you have prepared your body the right way and specifically for football. You can take that confidence—along with your new strength, speed and conditioning—onto the field and take the next step toward achieving your NFL dream.

HOW MUCH WEIGHT SHOULD I LIFT?

As a fitness and performance coach one of the most important questions I receive from athletes is how much weight they should lift for each exercise.

A rule of thumb here is to understand that the program is designed to increase three important aspects of performance: strength, muscle gain and muscle endurance. These are all important in training in the off season for football.

Strength is normally gained by lifting heavy weight and keeping a rep range of 1 to 6 reps.

Muscle gain has a medium weight to light weight rule and has a rep range of 8 to 12.

Muscle endurance is typically light weight to medium weight with a rep range of 15+.

One of the key and critical components of performance training for football is to know your body and what your pace is. The workouts are designed to take care of everything but weight.

Understand that weight is important but only after your technique is perfected.

Let's start Week 1 with minimal weight. As an example, anything that involves using a barbell should be done with no weight on the bar. After your technique is perfected, which can be after the first set, increase the weight by five pounds.

The same rule applies for every other exercise. Dumbbells, kettlebells and plates should be done initially at the lowest weight and slowly progress upward in weight. Bands should be used with the lowest resistance while progressing from the lowest to the highest. Medicine balls are also used progressing from lowest weight to highest. Box jumps and step-ups are first tried at the lowest height then progress to a higher height.

Knowing when you have the right weight is important. If you struggle to complete the exercise properly, then the weight is too heavy and you must drop it down. If you are completing the exercise too easily, then you should increase the weight. If you are completing a set slow and strenuous with great technique, then you have the right weight.

Remember there are no benefits to lifting large amounts of weight if you cannot perform the exercise movement correctly.

Good luck and train hard!

EQUIPMENT

Here is the list of equipment needed for the Nine Innovations workout. They all should be easily found at a gym or football training facility, or can be purchased at a sporting goods store. Where possible, substitutions can be made; for example, any markers could take the place of the cones. But overall, proper equipment—like proper technique— is key to getting the most out of the program.

- Barbells
- Kettlebells
- Dumbbells
- Plyo boxes
- Ab roller
- Resistance bands (all levels, including mini bands)
- Medicine balls (any weight)
- Valslides
- Airex pad
- Trap bar
- Battle ropes
- Mini hurdles (5)
- Cones (4)

- Speed/agility ladders
- Push sled
- Jungle gym/TRX bands
- Dead balls
- Stationary bike
- Pull-down machine
- Incline bench
- Peanut
- Trigger point
- Treadmill
- Tire
- Counter weights

As athletic trainers, we find that what we use to train in and with is just as important as our programs. Using the best equipment, apparel and products can help get athletes to the next level.

Starting from the ground up, care for our feet is essential for optimal training. There's no better sock for athletics than Injinji®. Its comfort and fit help to minimize those rubs from force application, which aids in eliminating blisters and unwanted foot problems.

Our choices in products and equipment are primarily from SKLZ® and Perform Better®. Their attention to what an athlete requires is second to none in performance. They build durable and dependable pieces for all the hard work athletes inflict on equipment.

We also highly recommend Powerblock®, which you see we use in some of the photos. Their simplicity and effectiveness can replace dumbbells at times.

Top-quality gear, such as Injinji® performance socks, help you as an athlete perform your best.

Hopefully these recommendations can help you train to be all that you can be as an athlete. Train hard!

DAILY WARM-UP

This is your daily warm-up. Every day, no matter what the focus is, even on the recovery day, this will be how you begin. It gets all the muscles stretched and activated to get the most out of the workout. It will be listed at the beginning of each week's chapter as well, as a reminder.

CORRECTIVES

FOAM ROLLER

- Roll your quads, hamstrings, glutes and calves over a foam roller.

ANKLE MOBILITY WITH BAND

- Wrap a band around the top of your toe and move your ankle to spell the letters A through G or rotate your ankles clockwise then counterclockwise.

KNEE MOBILITY
6 REPS EACH SIDE

- Stand on your left leg, move your right leg out in front of you and into the air while bending your left knee to do a single-legged squat.

HIP MOBILITY
6 TO 10 REPS EACH SIDE

- Bend one knee at 90 degrees and have the other knee on the ground.
- Pulse forward 6 to 10 times, switch knees and repeat.

THORACIC MOBILITY
10 REPS EACH SIDE

- Lie down on your back, bend your left leg and roll it over your body.
- With your right arm extended out and holding your left knee on the ground, bring your left arm up and rotate your body as far as you can.

SHOULDER MOBILITY
10 REPS

- Press your back against the wall, keeping the back of your heels against the wall.
- With your elbows bent, raise your arms toward the ceiling as far as possible while keeping your entire body against the wall.

GLUTE ACTIVATION
10 REPS EACH SIDE, THEN 10 WITH BOTH LEGS TOGETHER

- Wrap mini bands around your knees and ankles, and get down in a squat position without letting your knees go past your toes.
- Turn your right knee out, pushing against the band's resistance. Turn your right knee back in, then turn out your left knee. Finally, turn both knees out together.

MONSTER WALK STEPS

- Take large steps forward in a straight line for 10 yards.
- Walk backward the 10 yards.
- On your toes, sidestep 10 yards then back 10 yards one time down and back.

MOVEMENT

A SKIP

- With your knees high, skip for 10 yards, and then turn and come back.

B SKIP

- While skipping, straighten your leg and kick out for 10 yards, and then turn and come back.

BUTT KICKERS

- With your knee lifted into the air and forward, drive your heel into your butt for 10 yards, and then turn and come back.

QUICK FEET

- On your tiptoes, take small quick steps with arms moving slowly as if you're running.

- Go 5 yards, and then lightly jog 5 yards, turn back and repeat—5 yards quick steps and 5 yards light jog.

FALLING START

- On your toes, lean forward until you feel like you're going to fall, get into running position and drive yourself forward 20 to 25 yards in a light jog.

WATER BREAK

WEEK 1

Welcome to your first week of training! This is an opportunity to get better, improve your skills and make your mark on the field.

The first week of training will be new and different, but you should enjoy it and put everything you have into it. We will start with low reps and low circuits inside each block. Remember to use a challenging but comfortable amount of weight to complete your workout. The goal here is to get stronger, but we have to progress to heavy lifting—lifting a lot of weight doesn't matter if you can't translate it to your skill set.

Let's go! Train hard!

MONDAY

DAILY WARM-UP

- Refer to page 14.

MOVEMENT SERIES

SUICIDE SHUFFLE

- Place markers 5 yards apart to 25 yards (you can use football field lines).
- Shuffle sideways to the first marker 5 yards away and then sprint back to start.
- Shuffle sideways 10 yards and then sprint back to start.
- Shuffle sideways 15 yards and then sprint back to start.
- Shuffle sideways 20 yards and then sprint back to start.
- Shuffle sideways 25 yards and then sprint back to start.
- Do this once and then turn in the opposite direction and do it again.

CORE SERIES

PILLAR SERIES
20 SECONDS EACH POSITION

- Lie facedown on a bench with your waist at the end so your upper body is hanging over the edge, have a partner sit on your legs at your calves and hold yourself up even with the bench with your arms held to your side.
- With your partner still sitting on your legs at your calves, turn to the right, arms straight at your sides and hold yourself up even with the bench.
- With your partner still sitting on your legs at your calves, turn to the left, arms straight at your sides and hold yourself up even with the bench with your arms held to your side.
- Turn onto your back, have a partner sit on your legs at your shins, cross your arms across your chest and hold yourself up even with the bench.
- In all four parts of the series, make sure your body is straight and parallel to the ground, even with the bench.

BLOCK 1 (THREE CIRCUITS)

BARBELL HIGH PULL
8 REPS

- Grip a barbell outside your shoulder-width and hold it at your waist.
- Bend your knees and lean forward at the waist.
- Lower the bar to your knees and then quickly pull the bar up, bending your elbows and straightening your body while bringing the bar to shoulder height.

BARBELL STEP-UP
5 REPS EACH SIDE

- Hold a barbell on your shoulders behind your neck.
- Step up on a plyo box with your right leg, bend and bring up your left knee, and then step down with your left leg.
- Repeat stepping up with your right leg and bringing your left knee into the air.

DROP SQUAT TO BOX JUMP
5 REPS

- Stand behind a plyo box with your arms over your head.
- Swing your arms down past your body while bending slightly at the waist and knees, and jump onto the box.
- Step down.

AB ROLLOUT
10 REPS

- Start with your knees on an Airex pad, legs slightly separated and shins flat to the ground. Hold an ab roller directly in front of you and roll to full extension, and then roll it back.

BLOCK 2 (THREE CIRCUITS)

INCLINE BENCH (135 POUNDS)
10 REPS

- Lie back on an incline bench with your feet flat on the floor. Bring a bar down to your chest and back up.

BAND PUSH-UP
20 REPS

- Put a band under your palms and around your back across your shoulder blades. Do push-ups.

IPSILATERAL KETTLEBELL ROMANIAN DEAD LIFT
8 REPS

- Hold a kettlebell in your right hand. Bend at the waist and raise your left leg into the air behind you, keeping it straight. Touch the kettlebell to the ground and stand up.
- Switch and hold the kettlebell in your left hand. Bend at the waist and raise your right leg in the air behind you, keeping it straight. Touch the kettlebell to the ground and stand up.
- That is 1 rep.

LEG RAISES
15 REPS

- Hold on to a pull-up bar with a neutral grip and your arms toward the edges of the bar so your body makes a Y.
- Bend at the waist, pulling both legs up and out in front while keeping them together.

BLOCK 3 (TWO CIRCUITS)

BASE POSITION EXTENSION
8 REPS

- Tie an exercise band to equipment at about shoulder height. Stand far enough away that it is stretched out.
- With legs shoulder-width apart, knees and waist bent slightly and hands clasped together holding the band, straighten your arms, and then then pull them back.

HEAVY DUMBBELL ROW 1¼
10 REPS EACH ARM

- Hold a dumbbell in your left hand.
- Place your right arm on a dumbbell rack and bend at the waist with your right leg in front and feet shoulder-width apart.
- Bend your left elbow and bring the dumbbell all the way up to your body, straighten your arm, bring the dumbbell back up one-quarter of the way and lower it back down.

ROTATION OVERHEAD MEDICINE BALL SLAM
5 REPS

- With your feet shoulder-width apart, hold a medicine ball at waist height with bent elbows.
- Bring the ball around to the left, bending your knees slightly and turning your right heel out. Swing the ball over your head, and holding the ball with both hands, bring it down and slam it off the ground.
- Catch it on the bounce and swing it overhead to the right, bouncing it off the ground and catching it again.

X PULL DOWN
10 REPS

- With an exercise band attached to a pull-up bar, cross them and hold them with your arms extended at shoulder height.
- Pull both hands quickly down to the hips, and then bring them back up to the start position.

TUESDAY

DAILY WARM-UP

- Refer to page 14.

MOVEMENT SERIES

SINGLE-LEGGED HURDLES
3 REPS EACH LEG

- Place five mini hurdles one yard apart.
- Run over them with one foot landing between the hurdles on each step.

BOX DRILL WITH CONES

- Place four cones in a square, 5 yards apart.
- Sprint from cone A to cone B.
- Turn to the side and shuffle to cone C.
- Turn and run backward to cone D.
- Turn and sprint back to cone A.
- Then turn and go the other way, sprinting from A to D, etc.

LATERAL LADDER

- Lay a ladder out on the ground.
- Stand to the side of the ladder, face it and run, placing each foot in each space between the rungs and bringing it back outside the ladder, moving from one end to the other.

CORE SERIES

PUSH-UP SCAPULAR PILLAR SERIES
20 SECONDS, 10 SECONDS EACH POSITION

- Hold your body at the top push-up position for 20 seconds. Lower yourself to the floor, then make a Y with your arms straight, lifting your head, chest, arms and feet off the ground (hold hand weights for a greater challenge). Hold for 10 seconds.
- Lower your body, then move to the midpoint of a push-up and hold for 20 seconds. Lower yourself, then make a T with your arms straight, lifting your head, chest, arms and feet off the ground (hold hand weights for a greater challenge). Hold for 10 seconds.
- Lower your body, then move to the lowest point of a push-up and hold for 20 seconds. Lower yourself, then make a W with your arms, bending your elbows so your hands are at ear level and lifting your head, chest, arms and feet off the ground (hold hand weights for a greater challenge). Hold for 10 seconds. Lower your body.

BLOCK 1 (THREE CIRCUITS)

ROMANIAN DEAD LIFT TO POWER SHRUG
5 REPS

- Hold a bar with your arms extended straight down.
- Bend at the waist and knees until the bar is at mid-shins.
- Bring the bar up quickly, shrugging and lifting your heels off the ground.

BARBELL BAND BENCH
8 REPS (FIRST CIRCUIT), 6 REPS (SECOND), 4 REPS (THIRD)

- Attach a band from the bottom of a bench to each side of the bar.
- Bench press, bringing the bar all the way down to your chest and back up.

DUMBBELL PUSH-UP TO ROW
5 REPS

- Get in push-up position with your hands on the dumbbells.
- Do a full push-up, down and up.
- Bend your right arm up until the dumbbell is even with your ribs.
- Straighten your arm back down to the ground.
- Bend your left arm up until the dumbbell is even with your ribs.
- Straighten your arm back to the ground.

VALSLIDE HIP FLEXOR ABS
8 REPS EACH LEG

- Put each foot on a Valslide and rest your elbows, bent at 90 degrees, on a bench palms up.
- Alternate bending each knee up and sliding each foot as far as possible.

BLOCK 2 (THREE CIRCUITS)

REAR FOOT ELEVATED BARBELL BAND SPLIT SQUAT
5 REPS EACH SIDE

- Bend your right leg at the knee and put your right toes on the middle of a plyo box.
- Attach bands from the floor to the outside of a bar.
- With the bar resting across your back below the neck and your left foot slightly in front of your body, bend your left knee, dipping your right knee down and then lift up.
- Switch legs and repeat.

QUAD HIP FLEXOR STRETCH
6 REPS EACH SIDE

- Place your right knee bent on an Airex pad that is on the ground and rest the top of your right foot on a stability ball or bench so that the bottom of the foot is facing the ceiling. Your left leg should be in front in a bent position.
- Lean forward, bending your left knee forward and reaching your right arm diagonally into the air.

IPSILATERAL KETTLEBELL ROW
8 REPS EACH SIDE

- Hold a kettlebell, dumbbell or powerblock (shown in photos) in your right hand. Bend at the waist and raise your right leg into the air behind you, keeping it straight.
- Bend your right arm at the elbow, raise it as far as you can, straighten it and lower the kettlebell to the ground.
- After 8 reps, switch legs and repeat with the kettlebell in your left hand.

FACE PULL
15 REPS

- Attach a band to the top of a jungle gym so it's coming down at a 45-degree angle.
- Bend your knees and waist as if you're sitting down halfway.
- Bend your elbows, pull back the band toward your face and then straighten your arms.

BLOCK 3 (TWO CIRCUITS)

SINGLE-LEGGED SQUAT
8 REPS EACH LEG

- Stand with one foot on a plyo box and the other foot suspended in the air, and hold small counter weights in your hand.
- Squat slowly on the leg that is on the box. Use the counter weights to extend your arms in front of you.
- Go as low as you can and then straighten up.

SQUAT TO TRUCK DRIVER
6 REPS

- Stand straight and hold a large barbell weight in front of you with both hands.
- Squat and raise the weight.
- Hold the weight in front of you, knees and waist still bent, arms parallel to the ground and turn the weight like a steering wheel 90 degrees to the left then 90 degrees to the right.

SPLIT-STANCE MEDICINE BALL OVERHEAD SLAMS
5 REPS EACH SIDE

- With your right leg in front, bend your knee keeping your foot flat on the floor, and bend your left knee, balancing on your toes.
- Hold a medicine ball at your waist, bring the ball around in a circle left to right in front of your head, slam it onto the ground, catch it on the bounce and circle in the other direction.

HALF-KNEE CURL PRESS
5 REPS EACH LEG

- Rest one knee on an Airex pad on the floor and place the other at a 90-degree angle with your foot flat on the floor.
- Hold dumbbells at your side.
- Bend your elbows bringing the weights to your shoulders (curl) and then straighten your arms upward (press).
- Lower the dumbbells to your shoulders and then straighten your arms to your sides.

WEDNESDAY

DAILY WARM-UP

- Refer to page 14.

RECOVERY

- Use a foam roller to go over all your soft tissue.

THURSDAY

DAILY WARM-UP

- Refer to page 14.

MOVEMENT SERIES

SUICIDE SHUFFLE

- Place markers 5 yards apart to 25 yards (you can use football field lines).
- Shuffle sideways to the first marker 5 yards away and then sprint back to start.
- Shuffle sideways 10 yards and then sprint back to start.
- Shuffle sideways 15 yards and then sprint back to start.
- Shuffle sideways 20 yards and then sprint back to start.
- Shuffle sideways 25 yards and then sprint back to start.
- Do this once and then turn in the opposite direction and do it again.

CORE SERIES

ABDOMINAL MEDICINE BALL THROWS
10 REPS EACH POSITION

POSITION 1

- Sit on the ground about 1 foot from a wall with your side to the wall.
- Hold the medicine ball on the side of your body farthest from the wall.
- Bend your knees with a soft block held in between.
- Cross your feet and lift them off the ground.
- With your body bent almost in a sit-up position, throw the ball sideways against the wall, catch it and bring it back to the far side of your body before repeating.

POSITION 2

- Turn your body around and repeat the steps of position 1.

(continued)

ARIAN FOSTER

Running Back
6-1, 227 pounds
Past teams: Miami Dolphins, Houston Texans

I wanted something that would cater to my specific needs as a running back in the NFL, so I went to my brother, Abdul, to work out with his program. There are many benefits. Conditioning, for one. I can carry the load as a running back now. While other players get weaker as the game progresses, I keep my level of play. I also feel the strength and explosion from these workouts.

Since using this program, I have become a four-time Pro Bowler, led the league in rushing in 2010 and maintained a lengthy career in the NFL. The program helped me to rehab and return to play successfully after injuries. I swear by the Nine Innovations program and would recommend it to anyone.

POSITION 3

- Lie on your back with your knees bent and feet a few inches from the wall.
- Hold the medicine ball over your head.
- Throw the ball against the wall while doing a sit-up.
- Catch the ball off the wall when you're fully sitting up and lie back down.

BLOCK 1 (THREE CIRCUITS)

DUMBBELL SNATCH
5 REPS EACH ARM

- Standing straight, position your legs shoulder-width apart.
- Hold a dumbbell in your right hand, arm straight out at shoulder height.
- Slightly bend at the waist and knees and lower your straight arm until the dumbbell is between your legs, about even with your knees.
- In one motion, jump and lift the dumbbell with your straight arm over your head.

BARBELL BAND BENCH
15 SECONDS (FIRST CIRCUIT), 10 SECONDS (SECOND), 8 SECONDS (THIRD)

- Attach a band from the bottom of a bench to each side of a bar.
- Bench press, bringing the bar all the way down to your chest and back up as many times as possible in the allotted time.

MEDICINE BALL WALL CHEST THROWS
10 REPS

- Stand arm distance from the wall with your knees and waist slightly bent.
- Hold a medicine ball with your arms fully extended.
- Bring the ball to your chest, throw it into the wall and catch it when it bounces back.

MEDICINE BALL OVERHEAD THROWS
10 REPS

- Stand a few feet in front of a wall.
- Hold a medicine ball over your head, move your arms back a little and then forward to throw the ball against the wall.
- Catch the rebound.

BLOCK 2 (THREE CIRCUITS)

BARBELL BAND JUMP SQUAT
5 REPS (FIRST CIRCUIT), 7 REPS (SECOND), 9 REPS (THIRD)

- Attach bands from the Bottom of the rack to each side of a bar.
- With your feet shoulder-width apart and your hands positioned a little wider than your feet, rest the bar on the back of your neck.
- Stand straight and then squat and jump. Squat and jump for specified number of reps.

MEDICINE BALL SQUAT WALL THROW
5 REPS

- Stand a few feet from the wall and hold a medicine ball at your chest.
- Squat, then push up on your toes and throw the ball high off the wall. Let it hit the ground and then pick it up to throw again.

INCLINE DUMBBELL ROW
8 REPS

- Lie on your stomach on a bench inclined about 45 degrees.
- Hold the dumbbells with your arms straight down, then bend your elbows, pulling the weights up to your body and then lowering them back down.

BODY SAW
10 REPS

- Place your feet on Valslides and your elbows on an Airex pad with your body fully extended and held parallel to the ground. Elbows should be bent at a 90-degree angle and holding your body up, and your palms should be facing up.
- Without moving your elbows, use your arms to push your body back and pull it forward.

BLOCK 3 (TWO CIRCUITS)

SPLIT-STANCE MEDICINE BALL WALL THROW
10 REPS

- Stand perpendicular to a wall with your right leg in front, knee bent and foot flat on the floor, and your left leg back, knee bent and balancing on your toes.
- Hold a medicine ball at your waist, throw it sideways against the wall and catch the return.
- Switch legs and repeat.

LATERAL LUNGE WITH CURL
5 REPS

- Stand straight holding barbells at your sides.
- Take a step to the right with your right leg, toes pointing forward.
- Bend your right knee and waist, and bend your elbows to bring the weights to your shoulders and then straighten your arms.
- Return to a standing position and step to the left with your left leg, toes forward, left knee and waist bent, and curl the weights to your shoulders and then straighten.

DIPS
10 REPS

- With your hands on a dip bar, holding your body up, knees bent and ankles crossed, bend your elbows to lower your body and then straighten to return to the start position.

EGG CRADLES
10 REPS

- Lie on your back on the ground, bring your knees and feet together and your hands behind your head. Your elbows and knees should be together for the duration of the exercise.
- Have your partner hold your feet down on the floor.
- Rock your body up, keeping your body curled.
- Have your partner continue to hold your feet but let them rock up.

FRIDAY

DAILY WARM-UP

- Refer to page 14.

MOVEMENT SERIES

SINGLE-LEGGED HURDLES
3 REPS EACH LEG

- Place five mini hurdles one yard apart.
- Run over them with one foot landing between the hurdles on each step.

BOX DRILL WITH CONES

- Place four cones in a square, 5 yards apart.
- Sprint from cone A to cone B.
- Turn to the side and shuffle to cone C.
- Turn and run backward to cone D.
- Turn and sprint back to cone A.
- Then turn and go the other way, sprinting from A to D, etc.

LATERAL SINGLE-LEGGED LADDERS

- Lay a ladder out on the ground. Stand to the side of the ladder, face it and run, placing each foot in each space between the rungs and bringing it back outside the ladder, moving from one end to the other.

CORE SERIES

PAD PUNCHES
10 REPS EACH POSITION

POSITION 1

- Get into a sit-up position and have your partner hold an Airex pad even with your left hip and at a height so the middle of the pad is about shoulder height at the top of a sit-up. Do a sit-up, turn left and hit the pad with an open right hand.

POSITION 2

- Have your partner move to your right side.
- Do a sit-up, turn right and hit the pad with an open left hand.

POSITION 3

- Have your partner stand at your feet.
- Do a sit-up and hit the pad with both open hands.

BLOCK 1 (THREE CIRCUITS)

HANG CLEAN/FRONT SQUAT/OVERHEAD PRESS
3 REPS

- Stand with your feet shoulder-width apart, arms straight down, holding a bar at your hips.
- Lean slightly forward at your waist and bend your elbows to lift the bar to your shoulders.
- Do a squat with the bar at your shoulders.
- Straighten your arms and lift the bar over your head.
- Bring the bar back to your shoulders then to your waist.

TRAP BAR
6 REPS (FIRST CIRCUIT), 5 REPS (SECOND), 4 REPS (THIRD)

- Stand inside a trap bar, holding it with your arms straight down.
- Bend at your knees and waist, lowering the bar to just off the ground, and then stand back up.

QUAD HIP FLEXOR STRETCH
6 REPS EACH SIDE

- Place your right knee on an Airex pad that is on the ground and rest the top of your right foot on a stability ball or bench so that the bottom of the foot is facing the ceiling. Your left leg should be in front in a bent position.
- Lean forward, bending your left knee forward and reaching your right arm diagonally into the air.

HEAVY WEIGHTED ABS
15 REPS (START AT 35 POUNDS AND GO UP AS NEEDED)

- Get in a sit-up position with your arms bent holding a dumbbell or powerblock on your chest even with your shoulders.
- Do a sit-up, touching your elbows to your thighs and then going back down.

BLOCK 2 (THREE CIRCUITS)

VALSLIDE LUNGE
6 REPS EACH SIDE

- Stand straight with your right foot on an Airex pad and a Valslide under your left foot.
- Slide your left leg back, bending your right knee and lifting your arms up until your hands are in front of your face.
- When your left foot gets near to the farthest point, bend your left knee until it is just off the ground and then slide back to stand straight.

INCLINE BAND BENCH
5 REPS

- Attach a band from the bottom of a bench to each side of a bar.
- With the bench inclined, bench press, bringing the bar all the way down to your chest and back up.

ECCENTRIC NEUTRAL GRIP PULL-UPS
5 REPS

- Grip the bars that are perpendicular to the pull-up bar with your palms facing each other.
- Pull up until your head is over the bar and then take five seconds to lower yourself.

BATTLE ROPES
30 SECONDS

CHOOSE ONE OF THREE POSSIBILITIES

- Two-handed chops: Make chopping motions while holding the battle ropes, alternating your hands to make waves.

- Slams: Pick up and slam down the battle ropes with both hands.

- Wave lunges: Do two-handed chops while doing forward lunges.

BLOCK 3 (TWO CIRCUITS)

DUMBBELL BENCH 1½
20 SECONDS

- Lie on your back on a bench, knees bent over the end of the bench and feet flat on the ground.
- Hold the dumbbells with your elbows bent and the dumbbells at your side with your hands pointing upward.
- Straighten your arms all the way up, bring them all the way back down and then move them halfway up and back down.
- Do as many as you can in the allotted time.

DUMBBELL ROW 1½
20 SECONDS EACH ARM

- Hold a dumbbell in your left hand.
- Place your right arm on a dumbbell rack and bend at the waist with your right leg in front of the left and feet shoulder-width apart.
- Bend your left elbow and bring the dumbbell all the way up to your body, straighten your arm and then bring the dumbbell halfway up.
- Do as many as possible in the allotted time.

BICEP CURL
20 SECONDS

- Stand straight, holding a bar with your palms turned out.
- Bend your elbows, curling the bar to your chest.
- Do as many curls as possible in the allotted time.

TRICEPS PUSH DOWN
20 SECONDS

- Wrap a band around the top of a pull-up bar and bend your elbows at a 90-degree angle.
- Hold the band, straighten your arms and then bend your arms back to a 90-degree angle.
- Do as many as possible in the allotted time.

WEEK 2

Congratulations, you made it past that intro week! The first few days are usually the hardest part of training. Now that you understand the cluster system, we're going to continue to introduce you to the dynamic exercise routines that will help you out on the field.

In this week, we will continue with the same number of sets and blocks. I want you to slightly increase the weight by no more than 5 pounds on all major exercises. Remember to gauge your weight so you challenge yourself but can complete the exercise with proper form. Form is very important, so use the guides and keep pressing forward!

Train hard!

MONDAY

DAILY WARM-UP

- Refer to page 14.

MOVEMENT SERIES

SUICIDE SHUFFLE

- Place markers 5 yards apart to 25 yards (you can use football field lines).
- Shuffle sideways to the first marker 5 yards away and then sprint back to start.
- Shuffle sideways 10 yards and then sprint back to start.
- Shuffle sideways 15 yards and then sprint back to start.
- Shuffle sideways 20 yards and then sprint back to start.
- Shuffle sideways 25 yards and then sprint back to start.
- Do this once then turn in the opposite direction and do it again.

CORE SERIES

PILLAR SERIES
20 SECONDS EACH POSITION

- Lie facedown on a bench with your waist at the end so your upper body is hanging over the edge, have a partner sit on your legs at your calves and hold yourself up even with the bench with your arms held to your side.
- With your partner still sitting on your legs at your calves, turn to the right, arms straight at your sides and hold yourself up even with the bench.
- With your partner still sitting on your legs at your calves, turn to the left, arms straight at your sides and hold yourself up even with the bench.
- Turn onto your back, have a partner sit on your legs at your shins, cross your arms across your chest and hold yourself up even with the bench.
- In all four parts of the series, make sure your body is straight and parallel to the ground, even with the bench.

BLOCK 1 (THREE CIRCUITS)

BARBELL HIGH PULL
8 REPS

- Grip a barbell outside your shoulder-width and hold it at your waist.
- Bend your knees and lean forward at the waist.
- Lower the bar to your knees and then quickly pull the bar up, bending your elbows and straightening your body while bringing the bar to shoulder height.

FRONT FOOT ELEVATED VALSLIDE LUNGE
8 REPS EACH SIDE

- Stand straight with your right foot on an Airex pad and a Valslide under your left foot.
- Slide your left leg back, bending your right knee and lifting your arms up until your hands are in front of your face.
- When your left foot gets near to the farthest point, bend your left knee until it is just off the ground and then slide it back to stand straight.

QUAD HIP FLEXOR STRETCH
6 REPS EACH SIDE

- Place your right knee on an Airex pad that is on the ground and rest the top of your right foot on a stability ball or bench so that the bottom of the foot is facing the ceiling. Your left leg should be in front in a bent position.
- Lean forward, bending your left knee forward and reaching your right arm diagonally into the air.

PLATE SIT-UPS
15 REPS

- In the sit-up start position, hold a plate over your chest with straight arms.
- Do a sit-up and at the top of it, push your arms back so the plate is over your head.
- Lie back down while returning your arms to the starting position, holding the plate over your chest with your arms straight.

BLOCK 2 (THREE CIRCUITS)

ECCENTRIC NEUTRAL GRIP PULL-UPS
8 REPS

- Grip the bars that are perpendicular to the pull-up bar with your palms facing each other.
- Pull up until your head is over the bar and then take five seconds to lower yourself.

PARTNER BAND ROW
10 REPS EACH ARM

- With a partner holding the other side of the band and your elbows bent, pull back one arm at a time to row.
- If you don't have a partner, attach the band to stationary equipment.

SINGLE-LEGGED SQUAT
8 REPS EACH LEG

- Stand with one foot on a plyo box and the other foot suspended in the air, and hold small counter weights in your hand.
- Squat slowly on the leg that is on the box. Use the counter weights to extend your arms in front of you.
- Go as low as you can and then straighten up.

VALSLIDE HIP FLEXOR ABS
8 REPS EACH LEG

- Put each foot on a Valslide and rest your elbows, bent at 90 degrees, on a bench palms up.
- Alternate bending each knee up and sliding each foot as far as possible.

BLOCK 3 (TWO CIRCUITS)

DUMBBELL BROAD JUMP
5 REPS

- Hold a dumbbell in each hand and do a broad jump as you would do normally.

WIDE-LEGGED SEATED KETTLEBELL ROTATIONAL PRESS
8 REPS

- Sit with your legs spread into a wide V in front of you.
- Hold a kettlebell in each hand at shoulder height with bent elbows.
- Straighten your right arm up and out, in front of your head on a diagonal.
- Bring it down and repeat with the opposite arm.

SPLIT-STANCE MEDICINE OVERHEAD BALL SLAMS
5 REPS EACH SIDE

- With your right leg in front, bend your knee keeping your foot flat on the floor, and bend your left knee, balancing on your toes.
- Hold a medicine ball at your waist, bring the ball around in a circle left to right in front of your head, slam it onto the ground, catch it on the bounce and circle in the other direction.

LEG THROWS
10 REPS

- Lie on the ground with a partner standing above, feet at your shoulders.
- Wrap your arms around your partner's ankles and grab them. Keep your feet together and your legs as straight as possible.
- Raise both of your legs and have your partner push them down and off to the left.
- Raise your legs back up to your partner's hands and have him push them to the right.
- Raise your legs back up and have your partner push them straight down.

TUESDAY

DAILY WARM-UP

- Refer to page 14.

MOVEMENT SERIES

DOUBLE-LEGGED HURDLES
3 REPS

- Place five mini hurdles one yard apart.
- Run through placing both feet down between the hurdles.

3 CONE DRILL

- Place cones five yards apart in a reverse *L*.
- Run from cone A to cone B and back to cone A.
- Then run from cone A to cone B, around cone C and back to cone B and cone A.

LATERAL DOUBLE-LEGGED LADDERS

- Lay a ladder out on the ground.
- Stand facing the ladder and run stepping both feet in each space between the rungs and then back outside the ladder before going to the next space.

CORE SERIES

PUSH-UP SCAPULAR PILLAR SERIES
20 SECONDS, 10 SECONDS EACH POSITION

- Hold your body at the top push-up position for 20 seconds. Lower yourself to the floor, then make a Y with your arms straight, lifting your head, chest, arms and feet off the ground (hold hand weights for a greater challenge). Hold for 10 seconds.
- Lower your body, then move to the midpoint of a push-up and hold for 20 seconds. Lower yourself, then make a T with your arms straight, lifting your head, chest, arms and feet off the ground (hold hand weights for a greater challenge). Hold for 10 seconds.
- Lower your body, then move to the lowest point of a push-up and hold for 20 seconds. Lower yourself, then make a W with your arms, bending your elbows so your hands are at ear level and lifting your head, chest, arms and feet off the ground (hold hand weights for a greater challenge). Hold for 10 seconds. Lower your body.

BLOCK 1 (THREE CIRCUITS)

BARBELL CLEAN TO PRESS
5 REPS

- Stand straight and hold a barbell at your waist with straight arms.
- Jump and bend your knees, waist and elbows, bringing the barbell up to your shoulders with your palms facing upward.
- Straighten your body and lift the barbell straight over your head.

DUMBBELL BENCH HIPS OFF
8 REPS

- With only your head and shoulders on the bench, knees bent, feet flat on floor and a dumbbell in each hand, hold your arms straight up.
- Bend your elbow, bring the dumbbell to your shoulder and then straighten your arm, pressing the dumbbell back up.
- You can alternate arms or do them together.

PLATE PUSH-UP
10 REPS

- Set two barbell plates just outside of your hands.
- Do a push-up. When you come up, push to lift yourself off the ground, move your arms out and land with your hands on the plates.
- Do another push-up and lift yourself off the ground, moving your hands back to their original position.

LEG RAISES
15 REPS

- Hold on to a pull-up bar with a neutral grip and your arms toward the edges of the bar so your body makes a Y.
- Bend at the waist, pulling both legs up and out in front while keeping them together.

BLOCK 2 (THREE CIRCUITS)

LATERAL VALSLIDE LUNGE
8 REPS EACH SIDE

- Stand straight with right foot on an Airex pad and Valslide under your left foot.
- Slide your left leg out to left, bending your right knee and lifting your arms up until your hands are in front of your face.
- When your left foot gets near to the farthest point, slide it back.

ADDUCTOR STRETCH
6 REPS

- With your legs slightly wider than shoulder-width apart, and your knees on Airex pads, bend at the waist so your thighs are perpendicular to your lower legs and you're balanced on your elbows or fingertips, with your arms shoulder-width apart.
- Lean forward, straightening your body at the waist to feel the stretch.
- Hold for 30 seconds.

DUMBBELL PUSH-UP TO ROW
5 REPS

- Get in push-up position with your hands on the dumbbells.
- Do a full push-up, down and up.
- Bend your right arm up until the dumbbell is even with your ribs.
- Straighten your arm back down to the ground.
- Bend your left arm up until the dumbbell is even with your ribs.
- Straighten your arm back to the ground.

PLATE HOLDS
30 SECONDS

- Sit on the floor with your legs straight.
- Take a plate and lean back, lift your legs off the ground, bring the plate up with straight arms and hold it diagonally in front of your face.
- Hold for 30 seconds.

BLOCK 3 (TWO CIRCUITS)

LATERAL ROTATION BOX JUMPS
3 REPS EACH SIDE

- Stand about a foot from a plyo box with your legs shoulder-width apart.
- Raise your arms over your head, swing them down, bend your knees and bend forward at the waist.
- Swing your arms up and jump onto the box while turning 90 degrees so that you land facing to the right.

BAND ROTATION PULL/CHOP
10 REPS EACH SIDE

- Attach a band to a trap bar.
- Stand so the equipment is on your left side.
- Get in forward lunge position with your right leg back, knee bent, balanced on your toes, and your left knee bent almost 90 degrees with your foot flat on the floor.
- Hold the band with both hands.
- Pull down from your left shoulder to your right hip. Do not rotate your hips or torso.

REVERSE MEDICINE BALL WALL THROW
5 REPS

- Stand about two feet from a wall, facing away from the wall.
- Hold a medicine ball at your waist.
- Twist to the left, throw the ball off the wall and catch the rebound.
- Twist around to the right, throw the ball off the wall and catch the rebound.

VALSLIDE RUNNERS
20 SECONDS

- Start in the push-up position with Valslides under each foot.
- Alternate sliding one leg up toward your hands and then the other in a running motion.

WEDNESDAY

DAILY WARM-UP

- Refer to page 14.

RECOVERY

- Use a foam roller to go over all your soft tissue.

THURSDAY

DAILY WARM-UP

- Refer to page 14.

MOVEMENT SERIES

300-YARD SHUTTLE RUN

- Run 25 yards up and back six times.

CORE SERIES

SEATED MEDICINE BALL THROWS
THREE SETS OF 15 REPS

- From a seated position on the floor, throw a medicine ball back and forth with a partner two to three yards away.
- If there is no partner available, throw the ball against the wall.

BLOCK 1 (THREE CIRCUITS)

KETTLEBELL SWING
10 REPS

- Stand straight holding a kettlebell with both hands, arms straight in front of your body and legs shoulder-width apart.
- Bend your knees and swing the kettlebell through your legs then back up to shoulder height, keeping your arms straight.

KETTLEBELL SQUAT TO PRESS
10 REPS

- Hold two kettlebells at your chest with bent elbows and legs shoulder-width apart.
- Squat, bending at your knees and forward at your waist, and then come up and press the kettlebells over your head with straight arms.

GLOVER QUIN

Free Safety
#27 Detroit Lions
6-0, 207 pounds
Past team: Houston Texans

When you go to Nine Innovations, you are going to get stronger, faster, more explosive, quicker and in great shape! You will become tougher mentally because of the tough nature of the workouts.

I decided to go to Abdul because I wanted to get some good training and take my game to the next level. The training focused on the things I wanted to work on with my game and it has worked out perfectly.

My body composition has improved, allowing me to be able to move better and make more plays. Since I have been working out with this program, I have made it to the Pro Bowl, been named to the All-Pro team, led the NFL in interceptions and have been healthy and able to play in every game.

PUSH SLED

- Push a sled, running for 25 yards.

QUAD HIP FLEXOR STRETCH
6 REPS EACH SIDE

- Place your right knee on an Airex pad that is on the ground and rest the top of your right foot on a stability ball or bench so that the bottom of the foot is facing the ceiling. Your left leg should be in front in a bent position.
- Lean forward, bending your left knee forward and reaching your right arm diagonally into the air.

BLOCK 2 (THREE CIRCUITS)

DUMBBELL INCLINE BENCH REVERSE FLIES
12 REPS

- Lie on your stomach on an inclined bench with your head over the edge.
- Hold dumbbells in both hands with your arms extended straight toward the floor.
- Bring both arms up and back together with your elbows slightly bent and then back down toward the floor.

BULGARIAN SQUAT
8 REPS EACH SIDE

- Put your left foot up on a plyo box a few feet behind your right leg.
- Hold a kettlebell at your chest in both hands with your elbows bent.
- Bend at both knees, dipping your left knee down and keeping your torso straight.

TREADMILL PUSH
20 SECONDS

- Lean forward and hold the handles of a treadmill.
- With your feet toward the end of the treadmill, run while leaning toward the front of the treadmill, "pushing" forward with your feet.

MEDICINE BALL DOUBLE CRUNCH
15 REPS

- Lie on the floor holding a medicine ball over your head.
- Lift the ball up and lift your upper body off the ground while bending your knees, and bring them up to meet the ball.
- Keep the ball and feet off the ground throughout.

BLOCK 3 (TWO CIRCUITS)

DEAD BALL EXPLOSIVE WALL THROWS
3 REPS EACH SIDE

- Start down on your right knee bent at 90 degrees and your left foot on the ground.
- Position yourself about six feet from the wall.
- Push up on your left leg and take one big step toward the wall with your right while throwing the ball off of it.

SHOULDER 30S
10 REPS EACH POSITION

- Stand straight with your arms at your sides and a dumbbell in each hand.
- Lift your arms straight up at your sides to slightly above shoulder height and back down twice for 1 rep (lateral).
- Lift your arms straight up in front, palms down, to shoulder height and back down twice for 1 rep (frontal).
- Bend your knees and bend forward at the waist, bend your elbows slightly and bring your arms back and forward twice for 1 rep (flies).

STABILITY BALL HAMSTRING CURLS
12 REPS

- Lie on the ground with your arms out to the sides, palms down on ground and feet up on a stability ball.
- Lift your hips so everything but your head and shoulders are off the ground.
- Roll the ball toward your butt with your feet.

STABILITY BALL PLANKS
20 SECONDS

- Put your elbows and forearms on a stability ball, palms facing up.
- Put your body in plank position and get up on your toes.
- Hold this position for the allotted time.

FRIDAY

DAILY WARM-UP

- Refer to page 14.

MOVEMENT SERIES

DOUBLE-LEGGED HURDLES
3 REPS

- Place five mini hurdles one yard apart
- Run through placing both feet down between the hurdles.

3 CONE DRILL

- Place cones five yards apart in a reverse *L*.
- Run from cone A to cone B and back to cone A.
- Then run from cone A to cone B, around cone C and back to cone B and cone A.

LATERAL DOUBLE-LEGGED LADDERS

- Lay a ladder out on the ground.
- Stand facing the ladder and run stepping both feet in each space between the rungs and then back outside the ladder before going to the next space.

CORE SERIES

PAD PUNCHES
10 REPS EACH POSITION

POSITION 1

- Get into a sit-up position and have your partner hold an Airex pad even with your left hip and at a height so the middle of the pad is about shoulder height at the top of a sit-up. Do a sit-up, turn left and hit the pad with an open right hand.

(continued)

POSITION 2

- Have your partner move to your right side.
- Do a sit-up, turn right and hit the pad with an open left hand.

POSITION 3

- Have your partner stand at your feet.
- Do a sit-up and hit the pad with both open hands.

BLOCK 1 (THREE CIRCUITS)

BAND SQUAT
20 SECONDS

- Wrap two bands around stationary equipment at about foot height, then attach the other ends to either side of a barbell.
- Get under the barbell in traditional squat position and face away from the band.
- Bend at your knees and waist into a near sitting position and then straighten.
- Do as many as possible in the allotted time.

BIKE

- Bike as fast as possible for 20 seconds.

BARBELL BAND BENCH
20 SECONDS

- Attach a band from the bottom of a bench to each side of the bar.
- Bench press, bringing the bar all the way down to your chest and back up as many times as possible in the allotted time.

BAND ROW
20 SECONDS

- Wrap a band around stationary equipment at about waist height.
- Hold the ends in both hands, palms facing down.
- Bend at your knees and waist into a near sitting position that puts the band at chest height.
- Pull back, bending your elbows and turning your hands 90 degrees so your palms are facing each other.
- Pull all the way back until your hands are at your body and then straighten your arms again.
- Repeat for the allotted time.

BLOCK 2 (THREE CIRCUITS)

BAND SQUAT TO WRAP
20 SECONDS

- Wrap a band around stationary equipment at about knee height.
- Hold each end and face away from the band.
- Bend at your knees and waist into a near sitting position.
- Straighten your body and arms and bring them up and together, clapping in front of your face.
- Repeat for the allotted time.

BAND HIGH PULL
20 SECONDS

- Wrap a band around the base of a bench.
- Stand straight and hold both ends of the band with your palms facing down.
- Pull toward your face, bending your elbows straight out and finishing with your hands at your face and arms bent and at a 90-degree angle from your body before straightening your arms again.
- Repeat for the allotted time.

BAND BI (BICEP CURLS WITH BAND)
20 SECONDS

- Wrap a TRX band around the base of a bench or another stationary object.
- Stand straight and hold each handle of the band with your palms down.
- Bend your elbows up into a biceps curl while turning your hands until your palms are up.
- Straighten your arms back down.
- Repeat for the allotted time.

BAND TRI
20 SECONDS

- Wrap a band around a pull-up bar.
- Grip the band at each end with palms facing down.
- Straighten your arms in a downward motion, then slowly lift up.
- Repeat for the allotted time.

BLOCK 3 (TWO CIRCUITS)

BATTLE ROPES
20 SECONDS

CHOOSE ONE OF THREE POSSIBILITIES

- Two-handed chops: Make chopping motions while holding the battle ropes, alternating your hands to make waves.

- Slams: Pick up and slam down the battle ropes with both hands.

- Wave lunges: Do two-handed chops while doing forward lunges.

V-UPS
20 SECONDS

- Lie on your back, legs straight and arms over your head. For more of a challenge, hold a weighted medicine ball.
- Bend at the waist, touch your fingers or the ball to your toes to make a V shape (you can bend your knees slightly).
- Return to the start position.
- Do as many as you can in the allotted time.

PLANKS
20 SECONDS

- Hold your straight body off the ground, facing the floor, up on your toes, with elbows and forearms on the ground and palms up.
- Hold for the allotted time.

WEEK 3

Week two is in the books! Great work! Those circuits are tough, aren't they? But it's not a problem because you're getting stronger.

This is the last week of the conditioning phase of the program. Make sure you keep focusing on giving it your all and making every rep count. Stay at the same weight this week during the strength portion of the day and make sure your movement is consistent on times and effort.

Let's keep pushing through this week to the new phase.

Train hard!

MONDAY

DAILY WARM-UP

- Refer to page 14.

MOVEMENT SERIES

300-YARD SHUTTLE RUN

- Run 25 yards up and back six times.

CORE SERIES

PILLAR SERIES
20 SECONDS EACH POSITION

- Lie facedown on a bench with your waist at the end so your upper body is hanging over the edge, have a partner sit on your legs at your calves and hold yourself up even with the bench with your arms held to your side.
- With your partner still sitting on your legs at your calves, turn to the right, arms straight at your sides and hold yourself up even with the bench.
- With your partner still sitting on your legs at your calves, turn to the left, arms straight at your sides and hold yourself up even with the bench.
- Turn onto your back, have a partner sit on your legs at your shins, cross your arms across your chest and hold yourself up even with the bench.
- In all four parts of the series, make sure your body is straight and parallel to the ground, even with the bench.

BLOCK 1 (THREE CIRCUITS)

TWO-ARM KETTLEBELL HIGH PULL CLEAN AND SQUAT TO PRESS SERIES
3 REPS

- Stand straight with your legs shoulder-width apart, arms straight at your sides, holding a kettlebell in each hand.
- Bend forward at the waist and quickly bend your elbows and bring the kettlebells up to your shoulders keeping your palms facing your body and then straighten your arms back down.
- Lean forward a little bit, jump and bend your knees, bending your elbows and flipping the kettlebells on top of your shoulders with your palms up.
- Bend your knees and waist, and as you stand up, straighten your arms, pushing the kettlebells off your shoulders and straight over your head.

KETTLEBELL GOBLET SQUAT HOLDS
20 SECONDS

- Hold a kettlebell with both hands at about chin height.
- Bend at your knees and waist into a near sitting position and hold for the allotted time.

BAND RESISTANT LUNGE
3 REPS

- Wrap a band around your waist and attach it to a stationary object at waist-height or lower.
- Get in lunge position with your right leg bent almost 90 degrees, your foot flat on the floor, and your left leg back with knee bent nearly to floor and leg balanced on your toes.
- With your arms in running position—elbows bent, right arm back, left arm forward—jump and switch arms and legs into the opposite positions.

HEAVY WEIGHTED ABS
15 REPS (START AT 35 POUNDS AND GO UP AS NEEDED)

- Get in sit-up position with your arms bent holding a dumbbell or powerblock on your chest even with your shoulders.
- Do a sit-up, touching your elbows to your thighs and then going back down.

BLOCK 2 (THREE CIRCUITS)

INCLINE BAND BENCH
8 REPS

- Attach a band from the bottom of a bench to each side of a bar.
- With the bench inclined, bench press, bringing the bar all the way down to your chest and back up.

STANDING TS
6 REPS EACH LEG

- Get in forward lunge position with your right leg in front and left leg in back.
- Keep your waist and torso straight.
- Hold your arms straight and out to the side (like a T).
- Bring them together in front of your face and open them back up.

DEAD BALL SQUAT TO WALL THROW
5 REPS

- Hold a dead ball at your chest with your elbows bent and legs shoulder-width apart.
- Squat, bending at your knees and waist, and then come up and throw the dead ball against the wall.

EGG CRADLES
12 REPS

- Lie on your back on the ground, bring your knees and feet together and your hands behind your head. Your elbows and knees should be together for the duration of the exercise.
- Have your partner hold your feet down on the floor.
- Rock your body up, keeping your body curled.
- Have your partner continue to hold your feet but let them rock up.

BLOCK 3 (TWO CIRCUITS)

BOX JUMP TWO TO ONE
3 REPS EACH SIDE

- Stand a couple of feet from a plyo box, facing it.
- Swing your arms over your head and down past your sides while bending your knees and forward at the waist.
- Jump off of both feet and land on the box on your right foot.
- Do 3 reps and then repeat landing on your left foot.

REACTIVE MEDICINE BALL WALL THROW
5 REPS EACH SIDE

- Stand a few feet from a wall, bent slightly forward with your right shoulder facing the wall.
- Hold a medicine ball at your waist.
- Jump away from the wall, landing on your left foot with your right leg bent and in the air behind you.
- Jump back toward the wall, landing on your right foot, throw the ball sideways off the wall and catch the rebound.

OBLIQUE BAND ROTATION
10 REPS EACH SIDE

- Attach a band to stationary equipment at mid-torso height.
- Grab the end with both hands with your left shoulder facing where the band is attached.
- With straight arms, turn your torso and hips as far as you can to the right.
- Return to the starting point.

FARMER'S WALK
50 YARDS

- With kettlebells in each hand and arms at your sides, walk forward.

TUESDAY

DAILY WARM-UP

- Refer to page 14.

MOVEMENT SERIES

SINGLE- AND DOUBLE-LEGGED HURDLES
3 REPS

- Place 5 mini hurdles 1 yard apart.
- Run through placing each foot between the hurdles. (See pictures on page 23.)
- Then go through placing both feet between the hurdles. (See pictures on page 47.)

L DRILL WITH CONES

- Place three cones in an L shape five yards apart.
- Run from cone A to cone B, touch the ground and run back to cone A.
- Run from cone A around the outside of cone B and make a figure eight around cone C.
- Sprint back around the outside of cone B to cone A.

ICKY SHUFFLE LADDERS

- Lay out a ladder on the ground. Go through the ladder touching your left foot to the outside of each opening, both feet inside (right-left) and then your right foot out on the right side before moving on to the next one.

CORE SERIES

PUSH-UP SCAPULAR PILLAR SERIES
20 SECONDS, 10 SECONDS EACH POSITION

- Hold your body at the top push-up position for 20 seconds. Lower yourself to the floor, then make a Y with your arms straight, lifting your head, chest, arms and feet off the ground (hold hand weights for a greater challenge). Hold for 10 seconds.
- Lower your body, then move to the midpoint of a push-up and hold for 20 seconds. Lower yourself, then make a T with your arms straight, lifting your head, chest, arms and feet off the ground (hold hand weights for a greater challenge). Hold for 10 seconds.
- Lower your body, then move to the lowest point of a push-up and hold for 20 seconds. Lower yourself, then make a W with your arms, bending your elbows so your hands are at ear level and lifting your head, chest, arms and feet off the ground (hold hand weights for a greater challenge). Hold for 10 seconds. Lower your body.

BLOCK 1 (THREE CIRCUITS)

SINGLE-ARM DUMBBELL SNATCH TO PRESS
5 REPS EACH ARM

- Stand with your feet shoulder-width apart and a dumbbell horizontally between them.
- Bend down and grab the dumbbell with your right hand.
- In one motion, jump and lift the dumbbell over your head.
- Bend your elbow, bringing the dumbbell to your shoulder and then press it over your head, straightening your arm.
- Bend at the waist until the dumbbell touches the floor.

ROPE SLED PULL
25 YARDS

- Tie a rope to a sled. Stand with your feet shoulder-width apart, knees and waist bent slightly.
- Pull the sled in with a hand-over-hand rope pull.

HEAVY DUMBBELL ROW
5 REPS

- Hold a dumbbell in your left hand.
- Place your right arm on a dumbbell rack and bend at the waist with your right leg in front of the left and feet shoulder-width apart.
- Bend your left elbow and bring the dumbbell all the way up to your body and then straighten your arm.

LATERAL STRETCH
6 REPS

- Stand with your legs shoulder-width apart.
- Put your right arm on your hip, left arm over your head and bend your body to the right.
- Switch arms and bend your body to the left.

BLOCK 2 (THREE CIRCUITS)

DUMBBELL PULLOVER
10 REPS

  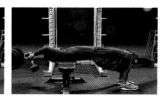

- With your shoulders, upper back and neck on a bench, set up perpendicular to it.
- Bend your knees at 90 degrees and keep your feet flat on the floor.
- Hold a dumbbell in both hands with straight arms over your chest.
- Lower your arms slowly as far back as they can go and then return them slowly to the start position.

SQUAT TO TRUCK DRIVER
8 REPS

- Stand straight and hold a large barbell weight in front of you with both hands.
- Squat and raise the weight.
- Hold the weight in front of you, knees and waist still bent, arms parallel to the ground and turn the weight like a steering wheel 90 degrees to the left then 90 degrees to the right.

DUMBBELL SIDE BENDS
15 REPS EACH SIDE

- Stand straight with your feet shoulder-width apart.
- Hold a dumbbell in your left hand at your side with your arm straight.
- Bend your right arm and hold your hand behind your head.
- Lean to the left a few inches.
- Lean back through, straight to the right side.

BLOCK 3 (TWO CIRCUITS)

DUMBBELL PUSH-UP TO ROW
5 REPS

- Get in push-up position with your hands on the dumbbells.
- Do a full push-up, down and up.
- Bend your right arm up until the dumbbell is even with your ribs.
- Straighten your arm back down to the ground.
- Bend your left arm up until the dumbbell is even with your ribs.
- Straighten your arm back to the ground.

BAND ROW
20 SECONDS

- Wrap a band around stationary equipment at about waist height.
- Hold the ends in both hands with your palms facing down.
- Bend at your knees and waist into a near sitting position that puts the band at chest height.
- Pull back, bending your elbows and turning your hands 90 degrees so your palms are facing each other.
- Pull all the way back until your hands are at your body and then straighten your arms again.
- Repeat for the allotted time.

MEDICINE BALL PARALLEL WALL THROW
10 REPS

- Stand a few feet from a wall and face the wall holding a medicine ball in both hands at your waist.
- Bend your knees and waist, holding the ball in both hands and swinging it around to your right side. Throw it against the wall and catch it.
- Bend your knees and waist, swing the ball to your left side with both arms. Throw it against the wall and catch it.

PLANK WALKS
25 YARDS

- Put Valslides under the toes of both feet and get in push-up position.
- Walk forward with hands, allowing feet to just slide behind.

WEDNESDAY

DAILY WARM-UP

- Refer to page 14.

RECOVERY

- Use a foam roller to go over all your soft tissue.

ANDRE JOHNSON

Wide Receiver
#81 Tennessee Titans
6-3, 229 pounds
Past teams: Houston Texans, Indianapolis Colts

I decided to train with Abdul and Nine Innovations because I was looking for something intense. This fit the description.

It's also an interesting approach; it focuses on what I'm already good at while enhancing the areas in which I'm lacking. As time goes on in your career you figure out what it is you need and don't need. This program has helped me do that and improve where I needed it.

THURSDAY

DAILY WARM-UP

- Refer to page 14.

MOVEMENT SERIES

300-YARD SHUTTLE RUN

- Run 25 yards up and back six times.

CORE SERIES

SEATED MEDICINE BALL THROWS
10 REPS

- From a seated position on the floor, throw a medicine ball back and forth with a partner two to three yards away.
- If there is no partner available, throw the ball against the wall.

BLOCK 1 (THREE CIRCUITS)

RDL TO HIGH PULL
8 REPS

- Stand with your feet shoulder-width apart holding a bar wider than your shoulders.
- Keep your arms straight, slightly bend your knees and waist and lower the bar to the ground.
- Quickly stand up, shrug your shoulders and rise up on your toes while bending your elbows and bringing the bar to chest level and then lower the bar back to the start position.

BAND SQUAT
8 REPS

- Wrap two bands around stationary equipment at about foot height, then attach the other ends to either side of a barbell.
- Get under the barbell in traditional squat position and face away from the band.
- Bend at your knees and waist into a near sitting position and then straighten.

SUMO SQUAT TO HAMSTRING STRETCH
6 REPS

- Bend at your knees and waist until you can grab your toes with both hands.
- Bend your knees farther and lower your butt toward the ground.
- Straighten your legs while still holding your toes.

SNATCH GRIP ABS
15 REPS

- Get in sit-up start position and hold a barbell over your chest.
- Do a sit-up, hold the barbell over your head at the height of the sit-up.
- Come back down, holding the bar with straight arms and finishing with your back on the ground and the bar again above your chest.

BLOCK 2 (THREE CIRCUITS)

INCLINE ALTERNATING DUMBBELL BENCH
8 REPS

- Lie back on an inclined bench with your feet flat on the floor.
- Hold a dumbbell in each hand with your arms straight up in the air.
- Bend your right elbow and bring the dumbbell to your body and then straighten your arm and press the dumbbell back into the start position.
- Bend your left elbow and bring the dumbbell to your body and then straighten your arm and press the dumbbell back into the start position.
- That is 1 rep.

PAD PUSH-UP
10 REPS

- With both hands on an Airex pad, do a push-up.

STABILITY BALL HAMSTRING CURLS
8 REPS

- Lie on the ground with your arms out to the sides, palms down on the ground and feet up on a stability ball.
- Lift your hips so everything but your head and shoulders are off the ground.
- Roll the ball toward your butt with your feet.

BODY SAW
12 REPS

- Place your feet on Valslides and your elbows on an Airex pad with your body fully extended and held parallel to the ground. Your elbows should be bent at a 90-degree angle, holding your body up, and your palms should be facing up.
- Without moving your elbows, use your arms to push your body back and then pull it forward.

BLOCK 3 (TWO CIRCUITS)

LATERAL ROTATION BOX JUMPS
3 REPS EACH SIDE

- Stand about a foot from a plyo box with your legs shoulder-width apart.
- Raise your arms over your head, swing them down, bend your knees and bend forward at the waist.
- Swing your arms up and jump up onto box, turning 90 degrees so you land facing to the right.

DEAD BALL SQUAT TO WALL THROW
5 REPS

- Hold a dead ball at your chest with elbows bent and legs shoulder-width apart.
- Squat, bending at your knees and waist, and then come up and throw the dead ball against the wall.

WIDE-LEGGED SEATED KETTLEBELL ROTATIONAL PRESS
8 REPS

- Sit with your legs spread into a wide V in front of you.
- Hold a kettlebell in each hand at shoulder height with bent elbows.
- Straighten your right arm up and out, in front of your head on a diagonal.
- Bring it down and repeat with the opposite arm.

VALSLIDE PIKES
15 REPS

- Put Valslides under each foot and get in push-up position.
- Slide your feet up together as far as you can then back down.

FRIDAY

DAILY WARM-UP

Refer to page 14.

MOVEMENT SERIES

SINGLE- AND DOUBLE-LEGGED HURDLES
3 REPS

- Place 5 mini hurdles 1 yard apart.
- Run through placing each foot between the hurdles. (See pictures on page 23.)
- Then run through placing both feet between the hurdles. (See pictures on page 47.)

L DRILL WITH CONES

- Place three cones in an *L* shape five yards apart.
- Run from cone A to cone B, touch the ground and run back to cone A.
- Run from cone A around the outside of cone B and make a figure eight around cone C.
- Sprint back around the outside of cone B to cone A.

ICKY SHUFFLE LADDERS

- Lay out a ladder on the ground. Go through the ladder touching your left foot to the outside of each opening, both feet inside (right-left) and then your right foot out on the right side before moving on to the next one.

CORE SERIES

PAD PUNCHES
10 REPS EACH POSITION

POSITION 1

• Get into a sit-up position and have your partner hold an Airex pad even with your left hip and at a height so the middle of the pad is about shoulder height at the top of a sit-up. Do a sit-up, turn left and hit the pad with an open right hand.

POSITION 2

• Have your partner move to your right side.

• Do a sit-up, turn right and hit the pad with an open left hand.

POSITION 3

• Have your partner stand at your feet. Do a sit-up and hit the pad with both open hands.

BLOCK 1 (THREE CIRCUITS)

BARBELL CLEAN, FORWARD LUNGE TO PRESS
3 REPS

- Stand straight and hold a barbell at your waist with your arms straight.
- Jump and bend your knees, waist and elbows, bringing the barbell up to your shoulders, gripping with your palms facing upward.
- Straighten your body and lunge—step forward with your right leg, bending your knee and dipping your left knee down.
- Step back then step forward with your left leg, bending your knee and dipping your right knee down.
- Step back to straighten.
- Lift the barbell straight over your head.

DUMBBELL BENCH SINGLE, SINGLE, DOUBLE
5 REPS

- Lie on a bench with your feet flat on the floor and a dumbbell in each hand.
- Bench press your right arm and bring it down.
- Bench press your left arm and bring it down.
- Bench press both arms together and bring them down.

FACE PULL
15 REPS

- Attach a band to the top of a jungle gym so it's coming down at a 45-degree angle.
- Bend your knees and waist as if you're sitting down halfway.
- Bend your elbows and pull back the band toward your face and then straighten your arms.

DOUBLE CRUNCH
15 REPS

- Lie on your back with your legs together and lift your feet a few inches off the ground.

- With your arms straight above your head and off the ground, bend your knees and bring your knees and upper body up so your arms meet your knees and then straighten back down, keeping your arms and feet off the ground throughout.

BLOCK 2 (THREE CIRCUITS)

LATERAL LUNGE TO PRESS
8 REPS EACH LEG

- Stand straight with your feet shoulder-width apart.
- Hold a barbell at your chest.
- Slide your left leg out straight, bending down with your right knee.
- Straighten your arms, pushing the barbell out, and then bend your elbows, bringing the barbell back to your chest.
- Slide your left leg back to the starting position.

ADDUCTOR STRETCH
6 REPS

- With your legs slightly wider than shoulder-width apart, and your knees on Airex pads, bend at the waist so your thighs are perpendicular to your lower legs and you're balanced on your elbows or fingertips, with your arms shoulder-width apart.
- Lean forward, straightening your body at the waist to feel the stretch.
- Hold for 30 seconds.

JUNGLE GYM (OR TRX) PUSH-UP
12 REPS

- Hold the handles at the bottom of hanging TRX bands on a jungle gym in push-up position, with your feet on a plyo box behind you.
- Do a push-up.
- When your arms are straight, bring your hands together, push them apart again and then lower them until your elbows are bent just past 90 degrees.

MEDICINE BALL PLANK HOLDS
20 SECONDS

- Put your elbows and forearms on a medicine ball with your palms facing up.
- Get in the plank position and up on your toes.
- Hold this position for the allotted time.

BLOCK 3 (TWO CIRCUITS)

MEDICINE BALL WALL CHEST THROWS
20 SECONDS

- Stand arm distance from the wall with your knees and waist slightly bent.
- Hold a medicine ball with your arms fully extended.
- Bring the ball to your chest, throw it into the wall and catch it when it bounces back.

JUNGLE GYM (OR TRX BAND) REVERSE FLIES
10 REPS

- With TRX bands hanging down from the top of equipment, grab a handle with each hand and lean all the way back until you're balancing on your heels.
- Keep your arms straight and the handles even with your shoulders.
- Pull up and push your arms out into a fly, keeping your toes off the ground.
- Lower back down.

MEDICINE BALL PERPENDICULAR WALL THROW
10 REPS EACH SIDE

- Stand perpendicular to the wall, your left shoulder nearest to it about two feet away.
- Hold a ball about stomach height.
- Bend at your knees and twist to the right, away from the wall.
- When turning back to the wall, throw the ball at it and catch the rebound.

SIT-UP TO ROTATIONAL PRESS
8 REPS

- Do a sit-up and at the height of the sit-up, extend your right arm diagonally up and across in front of your face and then bring it down.
- Extend your left arm and do the same.
- Lower back to the start position.

WEEK 4

Perfect! You made it through the conditioning phase of the program. You should be proud! These are not easy workouts, but if they were easy, everyone would do it.

Now we are stepping into the speed endurance phase of training. Some movement workouts will look familiar from the conditioning phase, because we have to continue to maintain our conditioning endurance in order to gain speed endurance. In the strength portion, we will begin to incorporate some metabolic work into our circuits.

Keep your weight the same again for this week; we still want to concentrate on form and technique—it's imperative for the later weeks in training.

Train hard!

MONDAY

DAILY WARM-UP

- Refer to page 14.

MOVEMENT SERIES

300-YARD SHUTTLE RUN

- Run 25 yards up and back six times.

CORE SERIES

PILLAR SERIES
20 SECONDS EACH POSITION

- Lie facedown on a bench with your waist at the end so your upper body is hanging over the edge, have a partner sit on your legs at your calves and hold yourself up even with the bench with your arms held to your side.
- With your partner still sitting on your legs at your calves, turn to the right, arms straight at your sides and hold yourself up even with the bench.
- With your partner still sitting on your legs at your calves, turn to the left, arms straight at your sides and hold yourself up even with the bench.
- Turn onto your back, have a partner sit on your legs at your shins, cross your arms across your chest and hold yourself up even with the bench.
- In all four parts of the series, make sure your body is straight and parallel to the ground, even with the bench.

BLOCK 1 (THREE CIRCUITS)

3-POSITION CLEAN
3 REPS

- Stand straight and hold a barbell with straight arms.
- Bend down a little until the barbell is at the top of your thigh.
- Jump slightly and bend your knees, waist and elbows, bringing the barbell up to your shoulders, gripping it so your palms are facing upward.
- Bring the barbell back down.
- Bend forward a little until the barbell is at the midpoint of your thigh.
- Jump slightly and bend your knees, waist and elbows, bringing the barbell up to your shoulders, gripping it so your palms are facing upward.
- Bring the barbell back down.
- Bend forward until the barbell is just below your knees.
- Jump slightly and bend your knees, waist and elbows, bringing the barbell up to your shoulders, gripping it so your palms are facing upward.
- Bring the barbell back down.

KETTLEBELL OFFSET FRONT SQUAT
8 REPS EACH SIDE

- Stand straight with your feet shoulder-width apart.
- Holding a kettlebell in your right hand, bend your right elbow completely and hold it at shoulder height perpendicular to your body.
- Hold your left arm straight out in front of you at shoulder height and bend your knees and waist into a sitting position.
- Stand back up.

BIKE
20 SECONDS

- Bike as fast as possible for the allotted time.

QUAD HIP FLEXOR STRETCH
6 REPS EACH SIDE

- Place your right knee on an Airex pad that is on the ground and rest the top of your right foot on a stability ball or bench so that the bottom of the foot is facing the ceiling. Your left leg should be in front in a bent postion.
- Lean forward, bending your left knee forward and reaching your right arm diagonally into the air.

BLOCK 2 (THREE CIRCUITS)

WALKING LUNGE WITH ROTATION
5 REPS

- Hold a medicine ball at your waist.
- Step forward with your right leg, bending your knee to 90 degrees and dipping your left knee down.
- Rotate your torso to the right and back to center.
- Step forward with your left leg, bending your knee to 90 degrees and dipping your right knee down.
- Rotate your torso to the left and back to center.
- That is 1 rep.

BARBELL BAND BENCH
5 REPS

- Attach a band from the bottom of a bench to each side of a bar.
- Bench press, bringing the bar all the way down to your chest and back up.

SHOULDER TAPS
20 SECONDS

- Get in push-up position.
- Lift your right hand and tap your left shoulder.
- Put your hand back down.
- Lift your left hand and tap your right shoulder.
- Put your hand back down.

SPLIT-STANCE DEAD BALL ROTATIONAL CHOP
5 REPS EACH SIDE

- Get in forward lunge position, your left leg forward and right leg back and balanced on your toes.
- Lift a dead ball with both hands and straighten arms across your body to above your left shoulder.
- Bring your straightened arms diagonally across your body in a chopping motion and throw the dead ball to the ground.

BLOCK 3 (TWO CIRCUITS)

GLUTE BRIDGE
20 SECONDS

- Lie on your back on the floor, knees bent, feet flat on the floor.
- With your arms straight down at your sides a little away from your body, your palms down and flat on the floor, raise your hips and toes as high as you can.
- Hold for the allotted time.

JUNGLE GYM (OR TRX) HAMSTRING CURLS 1¹/₂
5 REPS

- Put your feet in the TRX handles hanging on a jungle gym about six inches off the ground.
- Lie on your back with straight arms out from your sides and palms down on the floor.
- Bend both knees all the way, bringing your feet up toward your butt.
- Straighten.
- Bend halfway and straighten.

PUSH-UP WITH REACH
8 REPS EACH ARM

- Place a Valslide under your left hand and get in push-up position.
- Do a push-up, sliding your straightened left arm forward while bending your right elbow and lowering yourself toward the ground.
- Slide your left arm back while straightening your right arm.

TUESDAY

DAILY WARM-UP

- Refer to page 14.

MOVEMENT SERIES

SINGLE- AND DOUBLE-LEGGED HURDLES
3 REPS

- Place 5 mini hurdles 1 yard apart.
- Run through placing each foot between the hurdles. (See pictures on page 23.)
- Then run through placing both feet between the hurdles. (See pictures on page 47.)

BOX DRILL WITH CONES

- Place four cones in a square, 5 yards apart.
- Sprint from cone A to cone B.
- Turn to the side and shuffle to cone C.
- Turn and run backward to cone D.
- Turn and sprint back to cone A.
- Then turn and go the other way, sprinting from A to D, etc.

SKIER'S LADDER

- Place an agility ladder on the ground.
- From the bottom-center of the ladder, jump left to put your right foot in and left foot outside the ladder on the left side and then jump forward into the next one with your left foot in and right foot outside the ladder on the right side.
- Continue this alternating jumping pattern that mimics skiing until the end.

CORE SERIES

PUSH-UP SCAPULAR PILLAR SERIES

20 SECONDS, 10 SECONDS EACH POSITION

- Hold your body at the top push-up position for 20 seconds. Lower yourself to the floor, then make a Y with your arms straight, lifting your head, chest, arms and feet off the ground (hold hand weights for a greater challenge). Hold for 10 seconds.
- Lower your body, then move to the midpoint of a push-up and hold for 20 seconds. Lower yourself, then make a T with your arms straight, lifting your head, chest, arms and feet off the ground (hold hand weights for a greater challenge). Hold for 10 seconds.
- Lower your body, then move to the lowest point of a push-up and hold for 20 seconds. Lower yourself, then make a W with your arms, bending your elbows so your hands are at ear level and lifting your head, chest, arms and feet off the ground (hold hand weights for a greater challenge). Hold for 10 seconds. Lower your body.

BLOCK 1 (THREE CIRCUITS)

SINGLE-ARM DUMBBELL SNATCH TO PRESS
4 REPS EACH ARM

- Stand with your feet shoulder-width apart and a dumbbell horizontally between them.
- Bend down and grab the dumbbell with your right hand.
- In one motion, jump and lift the dumbbell over your head.
- Bend your elbow, bringing the dumbbell to your shoulder and then press it over your head, straightening your arm.
- Bend at the waist until the dumbbell touches the floor.

CONTRALATERAL ROW
8 REPS EACH SIDE

- Hold a dumbbell or powerblock in your right hand.
- Bend forward at your waist, lifting your straight right leg back until it's parallel with the ground. Your left leg can be slightly bent.
- Bend your right elbow, raising the dumbbell to your body, and then straighten.

SINGLE-ARM ALTERNATING KETTLEBELL SWING
8 REPS

- Stand straight with your feet shoulder-width apart.
- Hold a kettlebell in your right hand.
- Bending your knees, swing the kettlebell back between your legs, then up with a straight arm to shoulder height and switch hands at the top height.
- With the kettlebell in your left hand, swing it back between your legs and up high where you switch hands again.

BAND JUMP
5 REPS

- Attach one band to each side of the bottom of a barbell rack.
- Turn with your back toward the rack.
- Take the band from the right side, put the loop over your head and down on your left shoulder.
- Take the band from the left side, put the loop over your head and down on your right shoulder.
- Swing your arms up in front of your body, over your head with bent arms and then bring them down, bending your knees, and push off and jump.

BLOCK 2 (THREE CIRCUITS)

DEAD BALL TRANSVERSE LATERAL STEP-UP
8 REPS EACH SIDE

- Place a plyo box two feet behind you and to the left.
- Stand straight with your back to the box.
- Holding a dead ball with both hands at your chest, turn and step onto the box with your left leg.
- Bend your knee and bring your right leg up.
- Step back down.

MEDICINE BALL PUSH-UP
5 REPS

- With hands on a medicine ball, do a push-up.

SINGLE-LEGGED MEDICINE BALL SLAMS
8 REPS EACH LEG

- Stand straight, legs close together, holding a medicine ball at stomach level.
- Lift your left foot slightly off the ground.
- Raise the ball over your head and bring it down, bending at the waist and slamming it to the ground.

JUNGLE GYM (OR TRX) MARCHES
10 REPS

- Hold the handles of TRX bands that are hanging from a jungle gym at about chest height.
- Lean forward, keeping your arms straight.
- Bend your left knee up and then straighten it back down.
- Bend your right knee up and then straighten it back down.

BLOCK 3 (TWO CIRCUITS)

CLOSED GRIP BAND BENCH
20 SECONDS

- Hold a bar with your hands less than shoulder-width apart, no weight on the bar and not too much resistance on the band.
- Bring the bar down and back up as many times as possible in the allotted time.

SHOULDER 30S
10 REPS EACH POSITION

- Stand straight with your arms at your sides and a dumbbell in each hand.
- Lift your arms straight up at your sides to slightly above shoulder height and back down twice for 1 rep (lateral).
- Lift your arms straight up in front, palms down, to shoulder height and back down twice for 1 rep (frontal).
- Bend your knees and bend forward at the waist, bend your elbows slightly and bring your arms back and forward twice for 1 rep (flies).

LATERAL LUNGE
8 REPS

- Stand straight. Take a step to the right with your right leg, toes pointing forward.
- Bend your right knee and waist, keeping your left leg straight.
- Return to a standing position.
- Step to the left with your left leg, toes pointing forward.
- Bend your left knee and waist, keeping your right leg straight.
- Return to a standing position.

PUSH PLATE
25 YARDS

- Take a regular 45 plate, bumper or iron plate, put it on the ground flat and push for 25 yards.

WEDNESDAY

DAILY WARM-UP

- Refer to page 14.

RECOVERY

- Use a foam roller to go over all your soft tissue.

BRANDON LAFELL

Wide Receiver
#11 Cincinnati Bengals
6-3, 210 pounds
Past teams: Carolina Panthers, New England Patriots

I came to Abdul because I wanted something that challenged me to be a better player. This program does that for me. Nothing pushes me to my limit like this program.

Since I have been working with this program, I have felt better as an athlete and much more improved as a wide receiver. I have been on Super Bowl–winning teams and I know what it takes to become a better player. This program has aided in that.

I can work on my speed and gain strength all at the same time and I don't lose a step. As a Super Bowl champion, I believe in this program.

THURSDAY

DAILY WARM-UP

- Refer to page 14.

MOVEMENT SERIES

300-YARD SHUTTLE RUN

- Run 25 yards up and back six times.

CORE SERIES

SEATED MEDICINE BALL THROWS
10 REPS

- From a seated position on the floor, throw a medicine ball back and forth with a partner two to three yards away.
- If there is no partner available, throw the ball against the wall.

BLOCK 1 (THREE CIRCUITS)

DUMBBELL SQUAT TO JUMP
5 REPS

- Stand straight with your legs shoulder-width apart.
- With a dumbbell in each hand, bend your knees and waist into a sitting position.
- Stand back up and jump.

DUMBBELL REVERSE LUNGE TO KNEE DRIVE
8 REPS EACH LEG

- Stand straight with your legs close together, a dumbbell in each hand.
- Step back with your left leg, bending your right knee to 90 degrees and your left knee until it's nearly touching the ground.
- Lift your left foot and bring your leg forward, past the center and lift up your bent left knee as high as you can.

QUAD HIP FLEXOR STRETCH
6 REPS

- Place your right knee on an Airex pad that is on the ground and rest the top of your right foot on a stability ball or bench so that the bottom of the foot is facing the ceiling. Your left leg should be in front in a bent position.
- Lean forward, bending your left knee forward and reaching your right arm diagonally into the air.

RESISTED RUN
20 SECONDS

- Wrap a band around your waist and around a stationary object on the floor.
- Lean forward slightly and run for the allotted time.

BLOCK 2 (THREE CIRCUITS)

DUMBBELL SLIDE REACH TO ROW
5 REPS EACH ARM

- Place a Valslide under a dumbbell.
- Get in push-up position with your left hand holding the dumbbell.
- Go down for a push-up and slide your straight left arm forward while bending the right.
- Come up, sliding your left arm back to the start position.
- Bend your left elbow, pulling the dumbbell up to your body and putting it back down.

THREE-WAY PUSH-UP
5 REPS

- Get in the push-up start position with your left hand on a medicine ball.
- Do a push-up.
- Move the ball under your right hand and do a push-up.
- Roll the ball to the center, put both hands on it and do a push-up.
- That is 1 rep.

FRONT PLANK WITH ROW
10 REPS EACH ARM

- Get in plank position with your elbows and forearms on an Airex pad.
- Place your legs wider than shoulder-width apart.
- In your left hand, hold a TRX band that is attached to equipment a little above shoulder height (when in the plank position).
- Lift your left arm off the pad, straighten it at shoulder height with your palm down, then bend your elbow, twisting your hand so your palm is up and then pull the handle into your body.

BATTLE ROPES
20 SECONDS

CHOOSE ONE OF THREE POSSIBILITIES

- Two-handed chops: Make chopping motions while holding the battle ropes, alternating your hands to make waves.

- Slams: Pick up and slam down the battle ropes with both hands.

- Wave lunges: Do two-handed chops while doing forward lunges.

BLOCK 3 (TWO CIRCUITS)

SINGLE-LEGGED SQUAT WITH MEDICINE BALL EXTENSION
8 REPS

- Stand straight with your left foot at the edge of a plyo box and your right foot on the floor.
- Hold a medicine ball at your stomach.
- Do a squat, bending your left knee and waist while keeping your right leg straight.
- At the same time, straighten your arms to push the medicine ball out and then bring it back as you straighten your leg.

BARBELL CURL 1¹/₂
10 REPS

- Stand straight with your feet shoulder-width apart.
- Hold a barbell with your arms straight and palms up.
- Curl, bringing the barbell to your shoulders.
- Straighten your arms, bring the barbell back up halfway and then straighten to the start position.

RESISTED BACKPEDAL
10 TO 15 YARDS

- Use a partner or a resistance band long enough to wrap around your waist, and backpedal.

X PULL DOWN
15 REPS

- Attach bands to a pull-up bar, cross them and hold the ends.
- Stand facing a jungle gym with your feet shoulder-width apart.
- Straighten your arms, pulling all the way back behind your body, then bend your elbows and return to the starting position.

FRIDAY

DAILY WARM-UP

Refer to page 14.

MOVEMENT SERIES

SINGLE- AND DOUBLE-LEGGED HURDLES
3 REPS

- Place 5 mini hurdles 1 yard apart.
- Run through placing each foot between the hurdles. (See pictures on page 23.)
- Then run through placing both feet between the hurdles. (See pictures on page 47.)

BOX DRILL WITH CONES

- Place 4 cones in a square, 5 yards apart.
- Sprint from cone A to cone B.
- Turn to the side and shuffle to cone C.
- Turn and run backward to cone D.
- Turn and sprint back to cone A.
- Then turn and go the other way, sprinting from A to D, etc.

SKIER'S LADDER

- Place an agility ladder on the ground.
- From the bottom-center of the ladder, jump left to put your right foot in and left foot outside the ladder on the left side and then jump forward into the next one with your left foot in and right foot outside the ladder on the right side.
- Continue this alternating jumping pattern that mimics skiing until the end.

CORE SERIES

PAD PUNCHES
10 REPS EACH POSITION

POSITION 1

- Get into a sit-up position and have your partner hold an Airex pad even with your left hip and at a height so the middle of the pad is about shoulder height at the top of a sit-up. Do a sit-up, turn left and hit the pad with an open right hand.

POSITION 2

- Have your partner move to your right side.
- Do a sit-up, turn right and hit the pad with an open left hand.

POSITION 3

- Have your partner stand at your feet.
- Do a sit-up and hit the pad with both open hands.

BLOCK 1 (THREE CIRCUITS)

SNATCH GRIP HIGH PULL
5 REPS

- Stand straight with your legs slightly more than shoulder-width apart.
- Hold a barbell with your palms down and your hands about six inches wider than your hips.
- Bend forward at the waist and slightly at the knees, bend your elbows and quickly pull the barbell up to your chest and back down.

JUNGLE GYM WEIGHTED ROW
10 REPS

- In this exercise, your body is going to be parallel to the ground, elevated at bench level.
- Hang a TRX band so the handles are a foot above a bench or plyo box.
- Hold the handles and put your feet up on the bench or box, toes pointed toward the ceiling.
- Have a partner put a plate on your chest.
- Bend your arms and pull your straight body up to the band handles and lower yourself back down.

SNATCH GRIP ABS
15 REPS

- Get in sit-up start position and hold a barbell over your chest.
- Do a sit-up, hold the barbell over your head at the height of the sit-up.
- Come back down, holding the bar with straight arms and finishing with your back on the ground and the bar again above your chest.

PRETZEL STRETCH
6 REPS EACH SIDE

- Lie on the ground on your left side. With your right arm, grab your left ankle from behind you.
- Rest your right knee in front of you on the ground perpendicular with your torso.
- Hold your right knee to the ground with your left hand.
- Drive your right shoulder parallel to the ground behind you.

BLOCK 2 (THREE CIRCUITS)

FRONT FOOT ELEVATED SPLIT-STANCE ROW
10 REPS EACH SIDE

- Attach TRX bands to the top of a jungle gym or other stable equipment.
- Get in front lunge position with your right foot elevated on an Airex pad and your left leg back, balanced on your toes.
- Hold the handles of the bands with your palms down, and pull in toward your body, bending your elbows and twisting your hands 90 degrees so your palms turn toward your body.

KETTLEBELL PUSH/PULL
10 REPS EACH ARM

- Lie on a bench with a kettlebell in your right hand, elbow bent and the kettlebell at your shoulder.
- Hold the handle of a TRX band hanging from the jungle gym in your left hand with your palm toward your feet.
- Straighten your right arm, pushing the kettlebell toward the ceiling while pulling the band down to your body, twisting your hand 90 degrees so your palm is facing your body at the lowest point.

SINGLE-LEGGED BARBELL RDL
8 REPS ON EACH LEG

- Stand straight with your legs together, holding a barbell just below your waist.
- Keeping both legs straight, lift your left leg behind you while bending at the waist and lowering the bar to the floor.
- Straighten, returning your left leg to the floor.

PLANK WITH ROTATION
8 REPS

- Get in the plank position with your arms elevated on an Airex pad and turned so your forearms are perpendicular to your body.
- Lift your left arm up and rotate your body, straightening your arm so it ends up with your fingers pointing toward the ceiling.
- Bring your arm back down and repeat with your right arm.

BLOCK 3 (TWO CIRCUITS)

DUMBBELL BENCH 1½
20 SECONDS

- Lie on your back on a bench, knees bent over the end of the bench and feet flat on the ground.
- Hold the dumbbells with your elbows bent and the dumbbells at your side with your hands pointing upward.
- Straighten your arms all the way up, bring them all the way back down and then move them halfway up and back down.
- Do as many as you can in the allotted time.

DUMBBELL ROW
20 SECONDS EACH ARM

- Hold a dumbbell in your left hand.
- Place your right arm on a dumbbell rack and bend at the waist with your right leg in front of the left and feet shoulder-width apart.
- Bend your left elbow, bring the dumbbell all the way up to your body and then straighten your arm.
- Do as many as possible in the allotted time.

TRICEPS KICKBACK
20 SECONDS

- Attach a band to a bar on a bench or other stationary object.
- Stand a few feet away facing the bench, holding the ends of the band.
- Bend your knees slightly, bend at the waist and straighten your arms until they are extended fully behind your body, then return them to the starting position.
- Repeat as often as possible in the allotted time.

SUPINE BICEP CURLS
20 SECONDS

- Lie on your back on the floor.
- Attach a band to a dumbbell at your feet (you can also wrap the band around your feet).
- Hold the band and do as many bicep curls as you can in the allotted time.

WEEK 5

How was that opening week of speed endurance? Fun, right? Well, congratulations, you made it to week 5!

This week, we're going to ramp things up a bit for you. I want you to again increase the weight on your major exercises but by no more than five pounds. We are also going to add more reps to the circuits and one more circuit that is strictly metabolic. It's high intensity and designed to increase your heart rate and pull the rest out of you after the workout.

And don't forget to take that Wednesday and really recover.

Train hard!

MONDAY

DAILY WARM-UP

- Refer to page 14.

MOVEMENT SERIES

SUICIDE SHUFFLE

- Place markers 5 yards apart to 25 yards (you can use football field lines).
- Shuffle sideways to the first marker 5 yards away and then sprint back to start.
- Shuffle sideways 10 yards and then sprint back to start.
- Shuffle sideways 15 yards and then sprint back to start.
- Shuffle sideways 20 yards and then sprint back to start.
- Shuffle sideways 25 yards and then sprint back to start.
- Do this once and then turn in the opposite direction and do it again.

CORE SERIES

PILLAR SERIES
25 SECONDS EACH POSITION

- Lie facedown on a bench with your waist at the end so your upper body is hanging over the edge, have a partner sit on your legs at your calves and hold yourself up even with the bench with your arms held to your side.
- With your partner still sitting on your legs at your calves, turn to the right, arms straight at your sides and hold yourself up even with the bench.
- With your partner still sitting on your legs at your calves, turn to the left, arms straight at your sides and hold yourself up even with the bench.
- Turn onto your back, have a partner sit on your legs at your shins, cross your arms across your chest and hold yourself up even with the bench.
- In all four parts of the series, make sure your body is straight and parallel to the ground, even with the bench.

BLOCK 1 (THREE CIRCUITS)

DUMBBELL HIGH PULL
8 REPS

- Hold a dumbbell in each hand in front of your legs with your arms straight.
- Bend at your knees, and then when you're straightening your legs, bend your elbows and pull the dumbbells up to your chest and back down.

DUMBBELL STEP-UPS
8 REPS EACH LEG

- Holding a dumbbell in each hand, step onto a plyo box with your left leg and lift your right knee into the air.
- Step back down.

MEDICINE BALL SQUAT THROW
5 REPS

- Stand a few feet from the wall and hold a medicine ball at your chest.
- Squat, then push up on your toes and throw the ball high off the wall. Let it hit the ground and then pick it up to throw again.

HEAVY WEIGHTED ABS
15 REPS (START AT 35 POUNDS AND GO UP AS NEEDED)

- Get in sit-up position with your arms bent holding a dumbbell or powerblock on your chest even with your shoulders.
- Do a sit-up, touching your elbows to your thighs and then back down.

INCLINE DUMBBELL BENCH PRESS (135 POUNDS)
10 REPS

- Lie on your back on a bench with your knees bent at the end and your feet flat on the ground.
- Hold the dumbbells with your elbows bent and the dumbbells at your side, palms pointing upward.
- Straighten your arms all the way up, and then bring them all the way back down.

MEDICINE BALL PUSH-UP
15 REPS

- With hands on a medicine ball, do a push-up.

IPSILATERAL DUMBBELL RDL
8 REPS

- Hold a dumbbell in your right hand. Bend at the waist and raise your left leg into the air behind you, keeping it as straight as possible.
- Touch the dumbbell to the ground and then stand up.
- Switch and put the dumbbell in your left hand. Bend at the waist and raise your right leg in the air behind you, keeping it straight.
- Touch the dumbbell to the ground and then stand up.
- That is 1 rep.

WEIGHTED LEG RAISES
15 REPS

- Hold a pull-up bar at the ends and a dumbbell between your feet.
- Bend your knees toward your chest, lifting the dumbbell, and then straighten your legs.

BLOCK 3 (TWO CIRCUITS)

MEDICINE BALL RDL WALL THROW
6 REPS EACH LEG

- Stand about four feet from the wall, with your knees slightly bent.
- Hold a medicine ball at your waist.
- Bend forward at the waist, lifting your right leg into the air behind you, and lower the medicine ball to the ground.
- Bring your leg down and straighten it to the start position.
- Extend your arms, throwing the ball off the wall and catching it on the rebound.

HEAVY DUMBBELL ROW 1½
8 REPS EACH ARM

- Hold a dumbbell in your left hand.
- Place your right arm on a dumbbell rack and bend at the waist with your right leg in front and feet shoulder-width apart.
- Bend your left elbow and bring the dumbbell all the way up to your body, straighten your arm and then bring the dumbbell halfway up and lower it back down.

BAND ROTATION PULL/CHOP
8 REPS EACH SIDE

- Attach a band to a trap bar.
- Stand so the equipment is on your left side.
- Get in forward lunge position with your right leg back, knee bent, balanced on your toes, and your left knee bent almost 90 degrees with your foot flat on the floor.
- Hold the band with both hands.
- Pull down from your left shoulder to your right hip. Do not rotate your hips or torso.

PLANK ROW
10 REPS EACH ARM

- Attach a band to stable equipment about ankle height.
- In the plank position, with your elbows on an Airex pad, pull the band into your body with your left arm.

BATTLE ROPES
THREE SETS OF 30 SECONDS

CHOOSE ONE OF THREE POSSIBILITIES

- Two-handed chops: Make chopping motions while holding the battle ropes, alternating your hands to make waves.

- Slams: Pick up and slam down the battle ropes with both hands.

- Wave lunges: Do two-handed chops while doing forward lunges.

TUESDAY

DAILY WARM-UP

- Refer to page 14.

MOVEMENT SERIES

SLED SPRINT
50 YARDS

- Push a sled as fast as possible for 50 yards.

3 CONE DRILL

- Place cones five yards apart in a reverse *L*.
- Run from cone A to cone B and back to cone A.
- Then run from cone A to cone B, around cone C and back to cone B and cone A.

LATERAL SINGLE-LEGGED LADDERS

- Lay a ladder out on the ground. Stand to the side of the ladder, face it and run, placing each foot in each space between the rungs and bringing it back outside the ladder, moving from one end to the other.

CORE SERIES

PUSH-UP SCAPULAR PILLAR SERIES
25 SECONDS, 15 SECONDS EACH POSITION

- Hold your body at the top push-up position for 25 seconds. Lower yourself to the floor, then make a Y with your arms straight, lifting your head, chest, arms and feet off the ground (hold hand weights for a greater challenge). Hold for 15 seconds.
- Lower your body, then move to the midpoint of a push-up and hold for 25 seconds. Lower yourself, then make a T with your arms straight, lifting your head, chest, arms and feet off the ground (hold hand weights for a greater challenge). Hold for 15 seconds.
- Lower your body, then move to the lowest point of a push-up and hold for 25 seconds. Lower yourself, then make a W with your arms, bending your elbows so your hands are at ear level and lifting your head, chest, arms and feet off the ground (hold hand weights for a greater challenge). Hold for 15 seconds. Lower your body.

BLOCK 1 (THREE CIRCUITS)

DUMBBELL RDL TO SHRUG
5 REPS

- Stand with your feet a little more than shoulder-width apart and your knees slightly bent.
- Hold a dumbbell in each hand.
- Bend at the waist, lowering the dumbbells to about midshin.
- Straighten, then shrug your shoulders.

ALTERNATE DUMBBELL BENCH
8 REPS

- Lie on your back on a bench with your knees bent at the end and your feet flat on the ground.
- Hold the dumbbells with your elbows bent and the dumbbells at your side, palms pointing upward.
- Straighten your right arm all the way up, and then bring it all the way back down.
- Then straighten your left arm up, and bring it back down.

DUMBBELL PUSH-UP TO ROW
6 REPS

- Get in push-up position with your hands on the dumbbells.
- Do a full push-up, down and up.
- Bend your right arm up until the dumbbell is even with your ribs.
- Straighten your arm back down to the ground.
- Bend your left arm up until the dumbbell is even with your ribs.
- Straighten your arm back to the ground.

BLOCK 2 (THREE CIRCUITS)

REAR FOOT ELEVATED BARBELL BAND SPLIT SQUAT
6 REPS EACH SIDE

- Bend your right leg at the knee and put your right toes on the middle of a plyo box.
- Attach bands from the floor to the outside of a bar.
- With the bar resting across your back below the neck and your left foot slightly in front of your body, bend your left knee, dipping your right knee down and then lift up.

QUAD HIP FLEXOR STRETCH
6 REPS EACH SIDE

- Place your right knee bent on an Airex pad that is on the ground and rest the top of your right foot on a stability ball or bench so that the bottom of the foot is facing the ceiling. Your left leg should be in front in a bent position.
- Lean forward, bending your left knee forward and reaching your right arm diagonally into the air.

CONTRALATERAL ROW
8 REPS EACH SIDE

- Hold a dumbbell or powerblock in your right hand.
- Bend forward at your waist, lifting your straight right leg back until it's parallel with the ground. Your left leg can be slightly bent.
- Bend your right elbow, raising the dumbbell to your body, and then straighten.

DUMBBELL REVERSE FLIES
10 REPS

- Hold a dumbbell in each hand.
- Bend at your knees and waist with your arms hanging down and the dumbbells at about shin level.
- Bring both arms up to your shoulder height, arms straight, and then back down.

BLOCK 3 (THREE CIRCUITS)

SINGLE-LEGGED SQUAT
8 REPS EACH LEG

- Stand with one foot on a plyo box and the other foot suspended in the air, and hold small counter weights in your hand.
- Squat slowly on the leg that is on the box. Use the counter weights to extend your arms in front of you.
- Go as low as you can and then straighten up.

SQUAT TO TRUCK DRIVER
8 REPS

- Stand straight and hold a large barbell weight in front of you with both hands.
- Squat and raise the weight.
- Hold the weight in front of you, knees and waist still bent, arms parallel to the ground and turn the weight like a steering wheel 90 degrees to the left then 90 degrees to the right.

SPLIT-STANCE MEDICINE BALL OVERHEAD SLAMS
5 REPS EACH SIDE

- With your right leg forward, knee bent at 90 degrees, and your left leg back balanced on your toes in the lunge position, hold a medicine ball at your waist, then bring it around to the left, swing it over your head while holding the ball with both hands and come down and slam the ball off the ground.
- Catch the ball on the bounce and swing it over your head to the right, bouncing it off the ground and catching it again.

HALF-KNEE CURL PRESS
10 REPS EACH LEG FORWARD

- Rest one knee on an Airex pad on the floor and place the other at a 90-degree angle with your foot flat on the floor.
- Hold dumbbells at your side.
- Bend your elbows bringing the weights to your shoulders (curl) and then straighten your arms upward (press).
- Lower the dumbbells to your shoulders and then straighten your arms to your sides.

METABOLIC

BAND BI (BICEP CURLS WITH BAND)
THREE SETS OF 30 SECONDS

- Wrap a TRX band around the base of a bench or another stationary object.
- Stand straight and hold each handle of the band with your palms down.
- Bend your elbows up into a biceps curl while turning your hands until your palms are up.
- Straighten your arms back down.
- Repeat for the allotted time.

OWEN DANIELS

Tight End
6-3, 245 pounds
Past teams: Houston Texans, Baltimore Ravens, Denver Broncos

After having numerous surgeries on my knees, I needed a training program that catered to my rehabilitation and consistent strengthening that could also help me get better as a player and keep me improving.

I definitely got stronger in the areas I need to as a football player. I kept my strength as a tight end and improved my route running. I maintained my core strength, speed, agility and quickness.

I have been in the NFL for 10 years—spending a good bit of my career training at Nine Innovations—and this program has seen me through a Super Bowl victory with the Denver Broncos. I'm thankful for that.

WEDNESDAY

DAILY WARM-UP

- Refer to page 14.

RECOVERY

- Use a foam roller to go over all your soft tissue.

THURSDAY

DAILY WARM-UP

- Refer to page 14.

MOVEMENT SERIES

SUICIDE SHUFFLE

- Place markers 5 yards apart to 25 yards (you can use football field lines).
- Shuffle sideways to the first marker 5 yards away and then sprint back to start.
- Shuffle sideways 10 yards and then sprint back to start.
- Shuffle sideways 15 yards and then sprint back to start.
- Shuffle sideways 20 yards and then sprint back to start.
- Shuffle sideways 25 yards and then sprint back to start.
- Do this once and then turn in the opposite direction and do it again.

CORE SERIES

SEATED MEDICINE BALL THROWS
15 REPS

- From a seated position on the floor, throw a medicine ball back and forth with a partner two to three yards away. If there is no partner available, throw the ball against the wall.

BLOCK 1 (THREE CIRCUITS)

SINGLE-ARM DUMBBELL SNATCH
5 REPS EACH ARM

- Standing straight, position your legs shoulder-width apart.
- Hold a dumbbell in your right hand with your arm straight out at shoulder height.
- Slightly bend at the waist and knees, lowering your straight arm until the dumbbell is between your legs and about even with your knees.
- In one motion, jump and lift your straight arm over your head.

DUMBBELL BENCH
10 REPS

- Lie on your back on a bench with your knees bent at the end and your feet flat on the ground.
- Hold the dumbbells with your elbows bent and the dumbbells at your side, palms pointing upward.
- Straighten your arms all the way up and then bring them all the way back down.

WEIGHTED PULL-UPS
8 REPS

- Hold a pull-up bar with a neutral grip.
- Bend your knees to 90 degrees, keep your legs together and hold a dead ball between your legs or rest it on your thighs.
- Do a pull-up.

PLANKS
25 SECONDS

- Hold your straight body off the ground, facing the floor, up on your toes, with elbows and forearms on the ground and palms up.
- Hold for the allotted time.

BLOCK 2 (THREE CIRCUITS)

DUMBBELL SQUAT TO JUMP
5 REPS

- Stand straight with your legs shoulder-width apart.
- With a dumbbell in each hand, bend your knees and waist into a sitting position.
- Stand back up and jump.

MEDICINE BALL PARALLEL WALL THROW
10 REPS

- Stand a few feet from a wall and face the wall holding a medicine ball in both hands at your waist.
- Bend your knees and waist, holding the ball in both hands and swinging it around to your right side. Throw it against the wall and catch it.
- Bend your knees and waist, swing the ball to your left side with both arms. Throw it against the wall and catch it.

INCLINE DUMBBELL ROW
8 REPS

- Lie on your stomach on a bench inclined about 45 degrees.
- Hold the dumbbells with your arms straight down, then bend your elbows, pulling the weights up to your body and then lowering them back down.

BODY SAW
10 REPS

- Place your feet on Valslides and your elbows on an Airex pad with your body fully extended and held parallel to the ground. Elbows should be bent at a 90-degree angle and holding your body up, and your palms should be facing up.
- Without moving your elbows, use your arms to push your body back and pull it forward.

BLOCK 3 (THREE CIRCUITS)

BOX JUMP TWO TO ONE
3 REPS EACH SIDE

- Stand a couple of feet from a plyo box, facing it.
- Swing your arms over your head and down past your sides while bending your knees and forward at the waist.
- Jump off of both feet and land on the box on your right foot.
- Do 3 reps and then repeat landing on your left foot.

REACTIVE MEDICINE BALL WALL THROW
5 REPS EACH SIDE

- Stand a few feet from a wall, bent slightly forward with your right shoulder facing the wall.
- Hold a medicine ball at your waist.
- Jump away from the wall, landing on your left foot with your right leg bent and in the air behind you.
- Jump back toward the wall, landing on your right foot, throw the ball sideways off the wall and catch the rebound.

OBLIQUE BAND ROTATION
10 REPS EACH SIDE

- Attach a band to stationary equipment at mid-torso height.
- Grab the end with both hands with your left shoulder facing where band is attached.
- With straight arms, turn your torso and hips as far as you can to the right.
- Return to the starting point.

FARMER'S WALK
50 YARDS

- With kettlebells in each hand and arms at your sides, walk forward.

METABOLIC

INCLINE BAND FLIES
THREE SETS OF 30 SECONDS

- Wrap a band underneath the base of an incline bench, lie back on it and hold an end in each hand with your arms extended to the sides at chest height.
- Keeping your arms straight, bring your hands together then back out to the side.
- Do as many as possible in 30 seconds.

FRIDAY

DAILY WARM-UP

- Refer to page 14.

MOVEMENT SERIES

SLED SPRINT
50 YARDS

- Push a sled as fast as you can for 50 yards.

L DRILL WITH CONES

- Place three cones in an *L* shape five yards apart.
- Run from cone A to cone B and back.
- Run from cone A around the outside of cone B and make a figure eight around cone C.
- Sprint back around the outside of cone B to cone A.

LATERAL SINGLE-LEGGED LADDERS

- Lay a ladder out on the ground. Stand to the side of the ladder, face it and run, placing each foot in each space between the rungs and bringing it back outside the ladder, moving from one end to the other.

CORE SERIES

PAD PUNCHES
15 REPS EACH POSITION

POSITION 1

- Get into a sit-up position and have your partner hold an Airex pad even with your left hip and at a height so the middle of the pad is about shoulder height at the top of a sit-up. Do a sit-up, turn left and hit the pad with an open right hand.

(continued)

POSITION 2

- Have your partner move to your right side.
- Do a sit-up, turn right and hit the pad with an open left hand.

POSITION 3

- Have your partner stand at your feet.
- Do a sit-up and hit the pad with both open hands.

BLOCK 1 (THREE CIRCUITS)

DUMBBELL HANG CLEAN AND FRONT SQUAT
4 REPS

- Stand with your feet shoulder-width apart, arms straight and a dumbbell in each hand.
- Bend your knees and waist, pushing your butt back slightly and lowering the dumbbells.
- Jump and bend your elbows, bringing the dumbbells up to your shoulders.
- Straighten your arms back down.
- Do that twice, then bend your elbows and hold the dumbbells at your shoulders and do two front squats, bending your knees and waist, push your butt back into a sitting position and then straighten.

TRAP BAR
8 REPS (FIRST CIRCUIT), 6 REPS (SECOND), 4 REPS (THIRD)

- Stand inside a trap bar, holding it with your arms straight down.
- Bend at your knees and waist, lowering the bar just off the ground, and then stand back up.

PRETZEL STRETCH
6 REPS EACH SIDE

- Lie on the ground on your left side. With your right arm, grab your left ankle from behind you.
- Rest your right knee in front of you on the ground perpendicular with your torso.
- Hold your right knee to the ground with your left hand.
- Drive your right shoulder parallel to the ground behind you.

RUSSIAN TWIST
6 REPS

- Sit on the floor, on an Airex pad if you'd like.
- Bend your knees up, lean back a little and hold a medicine ball at your waist.
- Move your legs from side to side, lifting the ball over your body and banging the ball against the floor on either side of your hips.
- Do 6 reps (left and right side are 1 rep).

BLOCK 2 (THREE CIRCUITS)

LUNGE TWISTS
6 REPS EACH LEG

- Lunge forward and twist in the direction of the knee in front.

INCLINE DUMBBELL BENCH PRESS (135 POUNDS)
8 REPS

- Lie on your back on a bench with your knees bent at the end and your feet flat on the ground.
- Hold the dumbbells with your elbows bent and the dumbbells at your side, palms pointing upward.
- Straighten your arms all the way up, and then bring them all the way back down.

ECCENTRIC NEUTRAL GRIP PULL-UPS
5 REPS

- Grip the bars that are perpendicular to the pull-up bar with your palms facing each other.
- Pull up until your head is over the bar and then take five seconds to lower yourself.

BATTLE ROPES
25 SECONDS

CHOOSE ONE OF THREE POSSIBILITIES

- Two-handed chops: Make chopping motions while holding the battle ropes, alternating your hands to make waves.

- Slams: Pick up and slam down the battle ropes with both hands.

- Wave lunges: Do two-handed chops while doing forward lunges.

BLOCK 3 (THREE CIRCUITS)

DUMBBELL PUSH-UP TO ROW
5 REPS

- Get in push-up position with your hands on the dumbbells.
- Do a full push-up, down and up.
- Bend your right arm up until the dumbbell is even with your ribs.
- Straighten your arm back down to the ground.
- Bend your left arm up until the dumbbell is even with your ribs.
- Straighten your arm back to the ground.

BAND ROW
25 SECONDS

- Wrap a band around stationary equipment at about waist height.
- Hold the ends in both hands with your palms facing down.
- Bend at your knees and waist into a near sitting position that puts the band at chest height.
- Pull back, bending your elbows and turning your hands 90 degrees so your palms are facing each other.
- Pull all the way back until your hands are at your body and then straighten your arms again.
- Repeat for the allotted time.

MEDICINE BALL PARALLEL WALL THROW
10 REPS

- Stand a few feet from a wall and face the wall holding a medicine ball in both hands at your waist.
- Bend your knees and waist, holding the ball in both hands and swinging it around to your right side. Throw it against the wall and catch it.
- Bend your knees and waist, swing the ball to your left side with both arms. Throw it against the wall and catch it.

PLANK WALKS
25 YARDS

- Put Valslides under the toes of both feet and get in push-up position.
- Walk forward with hands, allowing feet to just slide behind.

METABOLIC

BAND ROW
THREE SETS OF 30 SECONDS

- Wrap a band around stationary equipment at about waist height.
- Hold the ends in both hands, palms facing down.
- Bend at your knees and waist into a near sitting position that puts the band at chest height.
- Pull back, bending your elbows and turning your hands 90 degrees so your palms are facing each other.
- Pull all the way back until your hands are at your body and then straighten your arms again.
- Repeat for the allotted time.

WEEK 6

Very good work! We're moving on to the last phase of speed endurance. Again, concentrate on technique and perfect movements. If the weight is too much and your technique begins to fail, take the weight down so you can focus on the technique.

We want to continue the same number of circuits and really drive home the movements in order to increase speed in the following week.

This week for recovery, make it active. Try yoga or simply wading in a pool or hot tub.

Let's keep up the work!

Train hard!

MONDAY

DAILY WARM-UP

- Refer to page 14.

MOVEMENT SERIES

300-YARD SHUTTLE RUN

- Run 25 yards up and back six times.

CORE SERIES

PILLAR SERIES
25 SECONDS EACH POSITION

- Lie facedown on a bench with your waist at the end so your upper body is hanging over the edge, have a partner sit on your legs at your calves and hold yourself up even with the bench with your arms held to your side.
- With your partner still sitting on your legs at your calves, turn to the right, arms straight at your sides and hold yourself up even with the bench.
- With your partner still sitting on your legs at your calves, turn to the left, arms straight at your sides and hold yourself up even with the bench.
- Turn onto your back, have a partner sit on your legs at your shins, cross your arms across your chest and hold yourself up even with the bench.
- In all four parts of the series, make sure your body is straight and parallel to the ground, even with the bench.

BLOCK 1 (THREE CIRCUITS)

3-POSITION CLEAN
3 REPS

- Stand straight and hold a barbell with straight arms.
- Bend down a little until the barbell is at the top of your thigh.
- Jump slightly and bend your knees, waist and elbows, bringing the barbell up to your shoulders, gripping it so your palms are facing upward.
- Bring the barbell back down.
- Bend forward a little until the barbell is at the midpoint of your thigh.
- Jump slightly and bend your knees, waist and elbows, bringing the barbell up to your shoulders, gripping it so your palms are facing upward.
- Bring the barbell back down.
- Bend forward until the barbell is just below your knees.
- Jump slightly and bend your knees, waist and elbows, bringing the barbell up to your shoulders, gripping it so your palms are facing upward.
- Bring the barbell back down.

KETTLEBELL OFFSET FRONT SQUAT
8 REPS EACH SIDE

- Stand straight with your feet shoulder-width apart.
- Holding a kettlebell in your right hand, bend your right elbow completely and hold it at shoulder height perpendicular to your body.
- Hold your left arm straight out in front of you at shoulder height and bend your knees and waist into a sitting position.
- Stand back up.

BIKE
25 SECONDS

- Bike as fast as possible for the allotted time.

QUAD HIP FLEXOR STRETCH
6 REPS EACH SIDE

- Place your right knee on an Airex pad that is on the ground and rest the top of your right foot on a stability ball or bench so that the bottom of the foot is facing the ceiling. Your left leg should be in front in a bent position.
- Lean forward, bending your left knee forward and reaching your right arm diagonally into the air.

BLOCK 2 (THREE CIRCUITS)

WALKING LUNGE WITH ROTATION
5 REPS

- Hold a medicine ball at your waist.
- Step forward with your right leg, bending your knee to 90 degrees and dipping your left knee down.
- Rotate your torso to the right and back to center.
- Step forward with your left leg, bending your knee to 90 degrees and dipping your right knee down.
- Rotate your torso to the left and back to center.
- That is 1 rep.

BARBELL BAND BENCH
5 REPS

- Attach a band from the bottom of a bench to each side of a bar.
- Bench press, bringing the bar all the way down to your chest and back up.

SHOULDER TAPS
25 SECONDS

- Get in a push-up position.
- Lift your right hand and tap your left shoulder.
- Put your hand back down.
- Lift your left hand and tap your right shoulder.
- Put your hand back down.
- Do as many times as possible in the allotted time.

SPLIT-STANCE DEAD BALL ROTATIONAL CHOP
5 REPS EACH SIDE

- Get in forward lunge position, your left leg forward and right leg back and balanced on your toes.
- Lift a dead ball with both hands and straighten arms across your body to above your left shoulder.
- Bring your straightened arms diagonally across your body in a chopping motion and throw the dead ball to the ground.

BLOCK 3 (THREE CIRCUITS)

GLUTE BRIDGE
25 SECONDS

- Lie on your back on the floor, knees bent, feet flat on the floor.
- With your arms straight down at your sides a little away from your body, your palms down and flat on the floor, raise your hips and toes as high as you can.
- Hold for the allotted time.

JUNGLE GYM (OR TRX) HAMSTRING CURLS 1½
5 REPS

- Put your feet in the TRX handles hanging on a jungle gym about six inches off the ground.
- Lie on your back with straight arms out from your sides and palms down on the floor.
- Bend both knees all the way, bringing your feet up toward your butt.
- Straighten.
- Bend halfway and straighten.

LEG LOWERING HAMSTRING STRETCH
6 REPS EACH LEG

- Wrap a band around your left foot and hold the other end.
- Lie on your back on the floor.
- Pull your left leg up as far as you can (your knee can be slightly bent).
- Lift your straight right leg so it's even with your left and then lower it.

PUSH-UP WITH REACH
8 REPS EACH ARM

- Place a Valslide under your left hand and get in push-up position.
- Do a push-up, sliding your straight left arm forward while bending your right elbow and lowering yourself toward the ground.
- Slide your left arm back while straightening your right arm.

METABOLIC

BATTLE ROPES
THREE SETS OF 30 SECONDS

CHOOSE ONE OF THREE POSSIBILITIES

- Two-handed chops: Make chopping motions while holding the battle ropes, alternating your hands to make waves.

- Slams: Pick up and slam down the battle ropes with both hands.

- Wave lunges: Do two-handed chops while doing forward lunges.

TUESDAY

DAILY WARM-UP

- Refer to page 14.

MOVEMENT SERIES

KNEELING SPRINTS
25 YARDS MAX, 5 TIMES EACH KNEE

- Get down on one knee, take off from that position and sprint up to 25 yards.
- Switch knees and sprint up to 25 yards.

L DRILL WITH CONES

- Place three cones in an *L* shape five yards apart.
- Run from cone A to cone B, touch the ground and run back to cone A.
- Run from cone A around the outside of cone B and make a figure eight around cone C.
- Sprint back around the outside of cone B to cone A.

LATERAL DOUBLE-LEGGED LADDERS

- Lay a ladder out on the ground.
- Stand facing the ladder and run stepping both feet in each space between the rungs and then back outside the ladder before going to the next space.

CORE SERIES

PUSH-UP SCAPULAR PILLAR SERIES
25 SECONDS. 15 SECONDS EACH POSITION

- Hold your body at the top push-up position for 25 seconds. Lower yourself to the floor, then make a Y with your arms straight, lifting your head, chest, arms and feet off the ground (hold hand weights for a greater challenge). Hold for 15 seconds.

- Lower your body, then move to the midpoint of a push-up and hold for 25 seconds. Lower yourself, then make a T with your arms straight, lifting your head, chest, arms and feet off the ground (hold hand weights for a greater challenge). Hold for 15 seconds.

- Lower your body, then move to the lowest point of a push-up and hold for 25 seconds. Lower yourself, then make a W with your arms, bending your elbows so your hands are at ear level and lifting your head, chest, arms and feet off the ground (hold hand weights for a greater challenge). Hold for 15 seconds. Lower your body.

BLOCK 1 (THREE CIRCUITS)

SINGLE-ARM DUMBBELL SNATCH TO PRESS
4 REPS EACH ARM

- Stand with your feet shoulder-width apart and a dumbbell horizontally between them.
- Bend down and grab the dumbbell with your right hand.
- In one motion, jump and lift the dumbbell over your head.
- Bend your elbow, bringing the dumbbell to your shoulder and then press it over your head, straightening your arm.
- Bend at the waist until the dumbbell touches the floor.

CONTRALATERAL ROW
8 REPS EACH SIDE

- Hold a dumbbell or powerblock in your right hand.
- Bend forward at your waist, lifting your straight right leg back until it's parallel with the ground. Your left leg can be slightly bent.
- Bend your right elbow, raising the dumbbell to your body, and then straighten.

SINGLE-ARM ALTERNATING KETTLEBELL SWING
8 REPS

- Stand straight with your feet shoulder-width apart.
- Hold a kettlebell in your right hand.
- Bending your knees, swing the kettlebell back between your legs, then up with a straight arm to shoulder height and switch hands at the top height.
- With the kettlebell in your left hand, swing it back between your legs and up high where you switch hands again.

BAND JUMP
5 REPS

  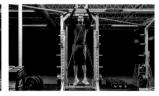

- Attach one band to each side of the bottom of a barbell rack.
- Turn with your back toward the rack.
- Take the band from the right side, put the loop over your head and down on your left shoulder.
- Take the band from the left side, put the loop over your head and down on your right shoulder.
- Swing your arms up in front of your body, over your head with bent arms and then bring them down, bending your knees, and push off and jump.

BLOCK 2 (THREE CIRCUITS)

TRANSVERSE STEP-UP MEDICINE BALL PUSH
8 REPS EACH SIDE

- Place a plyo box two feet behind you and to the right.
- Stand straight with your back to the box, holding a medicine ball at your stomach.
- Turn and step onto the box with your right leg.
- Bend your left knee and bring your left leg up.
- With your leg still in the air and with straight arms, push the medicine ball out, bring it back to your chest, lower your leg and step down.
- Do 8 reps then move to the other side of the box and step up with your left leg and repeat the steps lifting your right leg into the air.

MEDICINE BALL PUSH-UP
5 REPS

- With hands on a medicine ball, do a push-up.

SINGLE-LEGGED MEDICINE BALL SLAMS
8 REPS EACH LEG

- Stand straight, legs close together, holding a medicine ball at stomach level.
- Lift your left foot slightly off the ground.
- Raise the ball over your head and bring it down, bending at the waist and slamming it to the ground.

JUNGLE GYM (OR TRX) MARCHES
10 REPS

 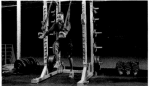

- Hold the handles of TRX bands that are hanging from a jungle gym at about chest height.
- Lean forward, keeping your arms straight.
- Bend your left knee up and then straighten it back down.
- Bend your right knee up and then straighten it back down.

BLOCK 3 (THREE CIRCUITS)

CLOSED GRIP BAND BENCH
25 SECONDS

- Hold a bar with your hands less than shoulder-width apart, no weight on the bar and not too much resistance on the band.
- Bring the bar down and back up as many times as possible in the allotted time.

SHOULDER 30S
10 REPS EACH POSITION

- Stand straight with your arms at your sides and a dumbbell in each hand.
- Lift your arms straight up at your sides to slightly above shoulder height and back down twice for 1 rep (lateral).
- Lift your arms straight up in front, palms down, to shoulder height and back down twice for 1 rep (frontal).
- Bend your knees and bend forward at the waist, bend your elbows slightly and bring your arms back and forward twice for 1 rep (flies).

LATERAL LUNGE
8 REPS

- Stand straight. Take a step to the right with your right leg, toes pointing forward.
- Bend your right knee and waist, keeping your left leg straight.
- Return to a standing position.
- Step to the left with your left leg, toes pointing forward.
- Bend your left knee and waist, keeping your right leg straight.
- Return to a standing position.

PUSH PLATE
25 YARDS

- Take a regular 45 plate, bumper or iron plate, put it on the ground flat and push it for 25 yards.

METABOLIC

BAND TRI
THREE SETS OF 30 SECONDS

- Wrap a band around a pull-up bar.
- Grip the band at each end with palms facing down.
- Straighten your arms in a downward motion, then slowly lift up.
- Repeat for the allotted time.

WEDNESDAY

DAILY WARM-UP

- Refer to page 14.

RECOVERY

- Use a foam roller to go over all your soft tissue.

JAMES IHEDIGBO

Strong Safety
#27 Buffalo Bills
6-1, 214 pounds
Past teams: New York Jets, New England Patriots, Baltimore Ravens, Detroit Lions

I choose the Nine Innovations program because it puts my body under the most stress, mentally and physically, which forces me to perform and fight through fatigue! That's where you make your biggest offseason gains.

This program is designed for speed, strength and explosiveness. I improve in all of these areas every year I have come to Nine and that's why I keep coming back.

After going to Nine the past three years, I put up some of the best stats in my NFL career. I put in the work in the off-season and then, toward the end of the year while everyone is getting weaker, I'm maintaining my strength, if not getting stronger.

As a 10-year NFL vet—and you can see from the veterans in the league that train here—everyone produces year in and year out. I don't think that's by chance. It's by work!

THURSDAY

DAILY WARM-UP

- Refer to page 14.

MOVEMENT SERIES

300-YARD SHUTTLE RUN

- Run 25 yards up and back six times.

CORE SERIES

SEATED MEDICINE BALL THROWS
THREE SETS OF 15 REPS

- From a seated position on the floor, throw a medicine ball back and forth with a partner two to three yards away.
- If there is no partner available, throw the ball against the wall.

BLOCK 1 (THREE CIRCUITS)

DUMBBELL SQUAT TO JUMP
5 REPS

- Stand straight with your legs shoulder-width apart.
- With a dumbbell in each hand, bend your knees and waist into a sitting position.
- Stand back up and jump.

DUMBBELL REVERSE LUNGE TO KNEE DRIVE
8 REPS EACH LEG

- Stand straight with your legs close together, a dumbbell in each hand.
- Step back with your left leg, bending your right knee to 90 degrees and your left knee until it's nearly touching the ground.
- Lift your left foot and bring your leg forward, past the center and lift up your bent left knee as high as you can.

QUAD HIP FLEXOR STRETCH
6 REPS EACH SIDE

- Place your right knee on an Airex pad that is on the ground and rest the top of your right foot on a stability ball or bench so that the bottom of the foot is facing the ceiling. Your left leg should be in front in a bent position.
- Lean forward, bending your left knee forward and reaching your right arm diagonally into the air.

RESISTED RUN
25 SECONDS

- Wrap a band around your waist and around a stationary object on the floor.
- Lean forward slightly and run for the allotted time.

BLOCK 2 (THREE CIRCUITS)

DUMBBELL SLIDE REACH TO ROW
5 REPS EACH ARM

- Place a Valslide under a dumbbell.
- Get in push-up position with your left hand holding the dumbbell.
- Go down for a push-up and slide your straight left arm forward while bending the right.
- Come up, sliding your left arm back to the start position.
- Bend your left elbow, pulling the dumbbell up to your body and putting it back down.

THREE-WAY PUSH-UP
5 REPS

- Get in the push-up start position with your left hand on a medicine ball.
- Do a push-up.
- Move the ball under your right hand and do a push-up.
- Roll the ball to the center, put both your hands on it and do a push-up.
- That is 1 rep.

FRONT PLANK WITH ROW
10 REPS EACH ARM

- Get in plank position with your elbows and forearms on an Airex pad.
- Place your legs wider than shoulder-width apart.
- In your left hand, hold a TRX band that is attached to equipment a little above shoulder height (when in the plank position).
- Lift your left arm off the pad, straighten it at shoulder height with your palm down, then bend your elbow, twisting your hand so your palm is up and then pull the handle into your body.

BATTLE ROPES
25 SECONDS

CHOOSE ONE OF THREE POSSIBILITIES

- Two-handed chops: Make chopping motions while holding the battle ropes, alternating your hands to make waves.

- Slams: Pick up and slam down the battle ropes with both hands.

- Wave lunges: Do two-handed chops while doing forward lunges.

BLOCK 3 (THREE CIRCUITS)

DUMBBELL BENCH 1¹/₂
25 SECONDS

- Lie on your back on a bench, knees bent over the end of the bench and feet flat on the ground.
- Hold the dumbbells with your elbows bent and the dumbbells at your side with your hands pointing upward.
- Straighten your arms all the way up, bring them all the way back down and then move them halfway up and back down.
- Do as many as you can in the allotted time.

DUMBBELL ROW
25 SECONDS EACH ARM

- Hold a dumbbell in your left hand.
- Place your right arm on a dumbbell rack and bend at the waist with your right leg in front of the left and feet shoulder-width apart.
- Bend your left elbow, bring the dumbbell all the way up to your body and then straighten your arm.
- Do as many as possible in the allotted time.

TRICEPS KICKBACK
25 SECONDS

- Attach a band to a bar on a bench or other stationary object.
- Stand a few feet away facing the bench, holding the ends of the band.
- Bend your knees slightly, bend at the waist and straighten your arms until they are extended fully behind your body, then return them to the starting position.
- Repeat as often as possible in the allotted time.

SUPINE BICEP CURLS
25 SECONDS

- Lie on your back on the floor.
- Attach a band to a dumbbell at your feet (you can also wrap the band around your feet).
- Hold the band and do as many bicep curls as you can in the allotted time.

METABOLIC

BAND SQUAT TO WRAP
3 SETS OF REPS OF 30 SECONDS

- Wrap a band around stationary equipment at about knee height.
- Hold each end and face away from the band.
- Bend at your knees and waist into a near sitting position.
- Straighten your body and arms and bring them up and together, clapping in front of your face.
- Repeat for the allotted time.

FRIDAY

DAILY WARM-UP

- Refer to page 14.

MOVEMENT SERIES

KNEELING SPRINTS
25 YARDS MAX, 5 TIMES EACH KNEE

- Get down on one knee, take off from that position and sprint up to 25 yards.
- Switch knees and sprint up to 25 yards.

L DRILL WITH CONES

- Place three cones in an *L* shape five yards apart.
- Run from cone A to cone B, touch the ground and run back to cone A.
- Run from cone A around the outside of cone B and make a figure eight around cone C.
- Sprint back around the outside of cone B to cone A.

LATERAL DOUBLE-LEGGED LADDERS

- Lay a ladder out on the ground.
- Stand facing the ladder and run stepping both feet in each space between the rungs and then back outside the ladder before going to the next space.

CORE SERIES

PAD PUNCHES
15 REPS EACH POSITION

POSITION 1

- Get into a sit-up position and have your partner hold an Airex pad even with your left hip and at a height so the middle of the pad is about shoulder height at the top of a sit-up. Do a sit-up, turn left and hit the pad with an open right hand.

POSITION 2

- Have your partner move to your right side.
- Do a sit-up, turn right and hit the pad with an open left hand.

POSITION 3

- Have your partner stand at your feet.
- Do a sit-up and hit the pad with both open hands.

BLOCK 1 (THREE CIRCUITS)

SNATCH GRIP HIGH PULL
5 REPS

- Stand straight with your legs slightly more than shoulder-width apart.
- Hold a barbell with your palms down and your hands about six inches wider than your hips.
- Bend forward at the waist and slightly at the knees, bend your elbows and quickly pull the barbell up to your chest and back down.

JUNGLE GYM WEIGHTED ROW
10 REPS

- In this exercise, your body is going to be parallel to the ground, elevated at bench level.
- Hang a TRX band so the handles are a foot above a bench or plyo box.
- Hold the handles and put your feet up on the bench or box, toes pointed toward the ceiling.
- Have a partner put a plate on your chest.
- Bend your arms and pull your straight body up to the band handles and lower yourself back down.

SNATCH GRIP ABS
15 REPS

- Get in sit-up start position and hold a barbell over your chest.
- Do a sit-up, hold the barbell over your head at the height of the sit-up.
- Come back down, holding the bar with straight arms and finishing with your back on the ground and the bar again above your chest.

PRETZEL STRETCH
6 REPS ON EACH SIDE

- Lie on the ground on your left side. With your right arm, grab your left ankle from behind you.
- Rest your right knee in front of you on the ground perpendicular with your torso.
- Hold your right knee to the ground with your left hand.
- Drive your right shoulder parallel to the ground behind you.

BLOCK 2 (THREE CIRCUITS)

FRONT FOOT ELEVATED SPLIT-STANCE ROW
10 REPS EACH SIDE

- Attach TRX bands to the top of a jungle gym or other stable equipment.
- Get in front lunge position with your right foot elevated on an Airex pad and your left leg back, balanced on your toes.
- Hold the handles of the bands with your palms down, and pull in toward your body, bending your elbows and twisting your hands 90 degrees so your palms turn toward your body.

SINGLE-LEGGED BARBELL RDL
8 REPS EACH LEG

- Stand straight with your legs together, holding a barbell just below your waist.
- Keeping both legs straight, lift your left leg behind you while bending at the waist and lowering the bar to the floor.
- Straighten, returning your left leg to the floor.

PLANK WITH ROTATION
8 REPS

- Get in the plank position with your arms elevated on an Airex pad and turned so your forearms are perpendicular to your body.
- Lift your left arm up and rotate your body, straightening your arm so it ends up with your fingers pointing toward the ceiling.
- Bring your arm back down and repeat with your right arm.

BLOCK 3 (THREE CIRCUITS)

DUMBBELL BENCH 1½
25 SECONDS

- Lie on your back on a bench with your knees bent at the end and your feet flat on the ground.
- Hold the dumbbells with your elbows bent and the dumbbells at your side, palms pointing upward.
- Straighten your arms all the way up, bring them all the way back down and then go halfway up and back down.
- Do as many as you can in the allotted time.

DUMBBELL ROW
25 SECONDS EACH SIDE

- Hold a dumbbell in your left hand.
- Place your right arm on a dumbbell rack and bend at the waist with your right leg in front of the left and feet shoulder-width apart.
- Bend your left elbow, bring the dumbbell all the way up to your body and then straighten your arm.
- Do as many as possible in the allotted time.

TRICEPS KICKBACK
25 SECONDS

- Attach a band to a bar on a bench or other stationary object.
- Stand a few feet away facing the bench and holding the ends of the band.
- Bend your knees slightly, bend at the waist and straighten your arms until they are extended fully behind your body, then return them to the starting position.
- Repeat as often as possible in the allotted time.

SUPINE BICEP CURLS
25 SECONDS

- Lie on your back on the floor.
- Attach a band to a dumbbell at your feet (you can also wrap the band around your feet).
- Hold the band and do as many bicep curls as you can in the allotted time.

METABOLIC

BAND SQUAT TO WRAP
3 SETS OF REPS OF 30 SECONDS

- Wrap a band around stationary equipment at about knee height.
- Hold each end and face away from the band.
- Bend at your knees and waist into a near sitting position.
- Straighten your body and arms and bring them up and together, clapping in front of your face.
- Repeat for the allotted time.

WEEK 7

We made it to Week 7! Phase three of the program is starting.

This week our focus will be on speed. Everything that we do will have a speed emphasis to it. We are going to continue our three-circuit workout, but this week we will increase the reps. If the weight can be upped without losing speed and technique, then go for it! If not, keep the weight the same.

Let's try to rest completely on Wednesday as we increase the speed and, possibly, the weight, too, this week.

Train hard!

MONDAY

DAILY WARM-UP

- Refer to page 14.

MOVEMENT SERIES

SUICIDE SHUFFLE

- Place markers 5 yards apart to 25 yards (you can use football field lines).
- Shuffle sideways to the first marker 5 yards away and then sprint back to start.
- Shuffle sideways 10 yards and then sprint back to start.
- Shuffle sideways 15 yards and then sprint back to start.
- Shuffle sideways 20 yards and then sprint back to start.
- Shuffle sideways 25 yards and then sprint back to start.
- Do this once and then turn in the opposite direction and do it again.

CORE SERIES

PILLAR SERIES
25 SECONDS EACH POSITION

- Lie facedown on a bench with your waist at the end so your upper body is hanging over the edge, have a partner sit on your legs at your calves and hold yourself up even with the bench with your arms held to your side.
- With your partner still sitting on your legs at your calves, turn to the right, arms straight at your sides and hold yourself up even with the bench.
- With your partner still sitting on your legs at your calves, turn to the left, arms straight at your sides and hold yourself up even with the bench.
- Turn onto your back, have a partner sit on your legs at your shins, cross your arms across your chest and hold yourself up even with the bench.
- In all four parts of the series, make sure your body is straight and parallel to the ground, even with the bench.

BLOCK 1 (THREE CIRCUITS)

BARBELL HIGH PULL
8 REPS

- Grip a barbell outside your shoulder-width and hold it at your waist.
- Bend your knees and lean forward at the waist.
- Lower the bar to your knees and then quickly pull the bar up, bending your elbows and straightening your body while bringing the bar to shoulder height.

FRONT FOOT ELEVATED VALSLIDE LUNGE
8 REPS EACH SIDE

- Stand straight with your right foot on an Airex pad and a Valslide under your left foot.
- Slide your left leg back, bending your right knee and lifting your arms up until your hands are in front of your face.
- When your left foot gets near to the farthest point, bend your left knee until it is just off the ground and then slide back to stand straight.

QUAD HIP FLEXOR STRETCH
6 REPS EACH SIDE

- Place your right knee bent on an Airex pad that is on the ground and rest the top of your right foot on a stability ball or bench so that the bottom of the foot is facing the ceiling. Your left leg should be in front in a bent position.
- Lean forward, bending your left knee forward and reaching your right arm diagonally into the air.

PLATE SIT-UPS
15 REPS

- In the sit-up start position, hold a plate over your chest with straight arms.
- Do a sit-up and at the top of it, push your arms back so the plate is over your head.
- Lie back down while returning your arms to the starting position, holding the plate over your chest with your arms straight.

BLOCK 2 (THREE CIRCUITS)

ECCENTRIC NEUTRAL GRIP PULL-UPS
8 REPS

- Grip the bars that are perpendicular to the pull-up bar with your palms facing each other.
- Pull up until your head is over the bar and then take five seconds to lower yourself.

PARTNER BAND ROW
10 REPS EACH ARM

- With a partner holding the other side of the band and your elbows bent, pull back one arm at a time to row.
- If you don't have a partner, attach the band to stationary equipment.

SINGLE-LEGGED SQUAT
8 REPS EACH LEG

- Stand with one foot on a plyo box and the other foot suspended in the air, and hold small counter weights in your hand.
- Squat slowly on the leg that is on the box. Use the counter weights to extend your arms in front of you.
- Go as low as you can and then straighten up.

VALSLIDE HIP FLEXOR ABS
8 REPS EACH SIDE

- Put each foot on a Valslide and rest elbows on a bench, bent at 90 degrees, palms up.
- Alternate bending each knee up and sliding each foot as far as possible.

BLOCK 3 (THREE CIRCUITS)

DEAD BALL BROAD JUMP
5 REPS

- Stand straight and hold a dead ball at your waist. With straight arms, swing the ball over your head.
- Bring it back down, into your stomach, bending your elbows, knees and waist to prepare to jump.
- Jump and push your arms straight in front of you, throwing the ball as you jump.

WIDE-LEGGED SEATED KETTLEBELL ROTATIONAL PRESS
8 REPS

- Sit with your legs spread into a wide V in front of you.
- Hold a kettlebell in each hand at shoulder height with bent elbows.
- Straighten your right arm up and out, in front of your head on a diagonal.
- Bring it down and repeat with the opposite arm.

SPLIT-STANCE MEDICINE BALL OVERHEAD SLAMS
5 REPS EACH SIDE

- With your right leg forward, knee bent at 90 degrees, and your left leg back balanced on your toes in the lunge position, hold a medicine ball at your waist, then bring it around to the left, swing it over your head while holding the ball with both hands and come down and slam the ball off the ground.
- Catch the ball on the bounce and swing it over your head to the right, bouncing it off the ground and catching it again.

LEG THROWS
15 REPS

- Lie on the ground with a partner standing above, feet at your shoulders.
- Wrap your arms around your partner's ankles and grab them. Keep your feet together and your legs as straight as possible.
- Raise both of your legs and have your partner push them down and off to the left.
- Raise your legs back up to your partner's hands and have him push them to the right.
- Raise your legs back up and have your partner push them straight down.

METABOLIC

SUPINE BICEPS
THREE SETS OF 30 SECONDS

- Lie on your back on a bench with your feet flat on the ground.
- Hold a dumbbell in each hand with your arms extended straight toward the ground below the bench.
- Bend your elbows and curl the dumbbells to your body height and then back down.
- Do as many as possible in the allotted time.

TUESDAY

DAILY WARM-UP

- Refer to page 14.

MOVEMENT SERIES

SINGLE- AND DOUBLE-LEGGED HURDLES
3 REPS

- Place 5 mini hurdles 1 yard apart.
- Run through placing each foot between the hurdles. (See pictures on page 23.)
- Then run through placing both feet between the hurdles. (See pictures on page 47.)

L DRILL WITH CONES

- Place three cones in an L shape five yards apart.
- Run from cone A to cone B, touch the ground and run back to cone A.
- Run from cone A around the outside of cone B and make a figure eight around cone C.
- Sprint back around the outside of cone B to cone A.

ICKY SHUFFLE LADDERS

- Lay out a ladder on the ground. Go through the ladder touching your left foot to the outside of each opening, both feet inside (right-left) and then your right foot out on the right side before moving on to the next one.

CORE SERIES

PUSH-UP SCAPULAR PILLAR SERIES
25 SECONDS, 15 SECONDS EACH POSITION

- Hold your body at the top push-up position for 25 seconds. Lower yourself to the floor, then make a Y with your arms straight, lifting your head, chest, arms and feet off the ground (hold hand weights for a greater challenge). Hold for 15 seconds.

- Lower your body, then move to the midpoint of a push-up and hold for 25 seconds. Lower yourself, then make a T with your arms straight, lifting your head, chest, arms and feet off the ground (hold hand weights for a greater challenge). Hold for 15 seconds.

- Lower your body, then move to the lowest point of a push-up and hold for 25 seconds. Lower yourself, then make a W with your arms, bending your elbows so your hands are at ear level and lifting your head, chest, arms and feet off the ground (hold hand weights for a greater challenge). Hold for 15 seconds. Lower your body.

BLOCK 1 (THREE CIRCUITS)

BARBELL CLEAN TO PRESS
5 REPS

- Stand straight and hold a barbell at your waist with straight arms.

- Jump and bend your knees, waist and elbows, bringing the barbell up to your shoulders with your palms facing upward.

- Straighten your body and lift the barbell straight over your head.

DUMBBELL BENCH HIPS OFF
8 REPS

- With only your head and shoulders on the bench, knees bent, feet flat on floor and a dumbbell in each hand, hold your arms straight up.
- Bend your elbow, bring the dumbbell to your shoulder and then straighten your arm, pressing the dumbbell back up.
- You can alternate arms or do them together.

PLATE PUSH-UP
10 REPS

- Set two barbell plates just outside of your hands.
- Do a push-up. When you come up, push to lift yourself off the ground, move your arms out and land with your hands on the plates.
- Do another push-up and lift yourself off the ground, moving your hands back to their original position.

LEG RAISES
15 REPS

- Hold on to a pull-up bar with a neutral grip and your arms toward the edges of the bar so your body makes a Y.
- Bend at the waist, pulling both legs up and out in front while keeping them together.

BLOCK 2 (THREE CIRCUITS)

LATERAL VALSLIDE LUNGE
8 REPS EACH SIDE

- Stand straight with right foot on an Airex pad and Valslide under your left foot.
- Slide your left leg out to left, bending your right knee and bending your arms up until your hands are in front of your face.
- When your left foot gets near to the farthest point, slide it back.

ADDUCTOR STRETCH
6 REPS

- With your legs slightly wider than shoulder-width apart, and your knees on Airex pads, bend at the waist so your thighs are perpendicular to your lower legs and you're balanced on your elbows or fingertips, with your arms shoulder-width apart.
- Lean forward, straightening your body at the waist to feel the stretch.
- Hold for 30 seconds.

DUMBBELL PUSH-UP TO ROW
5 REPS

- Get in push-up position with your hands on the dumbbells.
- Do a full push-up, down and up.
- Bend your right arm up until the dumbbell is even with your ribs.
- Straighten your arm back down to the ground.
- Bend your left arm up until the dumbbell is even with your ribs.
- Straighten your arm back to the ground.

PLATE HOLDS
25 SECONDS

- Sit on the floor with your legs straight.
- Take a plate and lean back, lift your legs off the ground, bring the plate up with straight arms and hold it diagonally in front of your face.
- Hold for 25 seconds.

BLOCK 3 (THREE CIRCUITS)

LATERAL ROTATION BOX JUMPS
3 REPS EACH SIDE

- Stand about a foot from a plyo box with your legs shoulder-width apart.
- Raise your arms over your head, swing them down, bend your knees and bend forward at the waist.
- Swing your arms up and jump up onto the box, turning 90 degrees so you land facing to the right.

BAND ROTATION PULL/CHOP
10 REPS EACH SIDE

- Attach a band to a trap bar.
- Stand so the equipment is on your left side.
- Get in forward lunge position with your right leg back, knee bent, balanced on your toes, and your left knee bent almost 90 degrees with your foot flat on the floor.
- Hold the band with both hands.
- Pull down from your left shoulder to your right hip. Do not rotate your hips or torso.

REVERSE MEDICINE BALL WALL THROW
5 REPS

- Stand about two feet from a wall, facing away from the wall.
- Hold a medicine ball at your waist.
- Twist to the left, throw the ball off the wall and catch the rebound.
- Twist around to the right, throw the ball off the wall and catch the rebound.

VALSLIDE RUNNERS
25 SECONDS

- Start in the push-up position with Valslides under each foot.
- Alternate sliding one leg up toward your hands and then the other in a running motion.

METABOLIC

TREADMILL SPRINTS
THREE SETS OF 30 SECONDS

- Sprint as fast as you can handle for the allotted time.

WEDNESDAY

DAILY WARM-UP

- Refer to page 14.

RECOVERY

- Use a foam roller to go over all your soft tissue.

THURSDAY

DAILY WARM-UP

- Refer to page 14.

MOVEMENT SERIES

SUICIDE SHUFFLE

- Place markers 5 yards apart to 25 yards (you can use football field lines).
- Shuffle sideways to the first marker 5 yards away and then sprint back to start.
- Shuffle sideways 10 yards and then sprint back to start.
- Shuffle sideways 15 yards and then sprint back to start.
- Shuffle sideways 20 yards and then sprint back to start.
- Shuffle sideways 25 yards and then sprint back to start.
- Do this once and then turn in the opposite direction and do it again.

CORE SERIES

SEATED MEDICINE BALL THROWS
THREE SETS OF 15 REPS

- From a seated position on the floor, throw a medicine ball back and forth with a partner two to three yards away.
- If there is no partner available, throw the ball against the wall.

BLOCK 1 (THREE CIRCUITS)

KETTLEBELL SWING
10 REPS

- Stand straight holding a kettlebell with both hands, arms straight in front of your body and legs shoulder-width apart.
- Bend your knees and swing the kettlebell through your legs and then back up to shoulder height, keeping your arms straight.

KETTLEBELL SQUAT TO PRESS
10 REPS

- Hold two kettlebells at your chest with bent elbows and legs shoulder-width apart.
- Squat, bending at your knees and forward at your waist, and then come up and press the kettlebells over your head with straight arms.

PUSH SLED
25 YARDS

- Push a sled, running for 25 yards.

DARIUS SLAY

Cornerback
#23 Detroit Lions
6-0, 190 pounds

I was looking for something that offered the entire all-around package: conditioning, strength training, speed, agility and quickness. That is everything I need in an off-season training program. Since I started with Nine Innovations, I've gained strength, I'm in great condition and my core is stronger. All of those have been a benefit to me and the position I play.

I'm ecstatic about what the program has done for me. I'm agile and strong. It has helped me be a better player for my team and helped me earn a contract extension with the Detroit Lions.

QUAD HIP FLEXOR STRETCH
6 REPS ON EACH SIDE

- Place your right knee bent on an Airex pad that is on the ground and rest the top of your right foot on a stabilty ball or bench so that the bottom of the foot is facing the ceiling. Your left leg should be in front in a bent position.
- Lean forward, bending your left knee forward and reaching your right arm diagonally into the air.

BLOCK 2 (THREE CIRCUITS)

DUMBBELL INCLINE BENCH REVERSE FLIES
12 REPS

- Lie on your stomach on an inclined bench with your head over the edge.
- Hold dumbbells in both hands with your arms extended straight toward the floor.
- Bring both arms up and back together with your elbows slightly bent and then back down toward the floor.

BULGARIAN SQUAT
8 REPS EACH SIDE

- Put your left foot up on a plyo box a few feet behind your right leg.
- Hold a kettlebell at your chest in both hands with your elbows bent.
- Bend at both knees, dipping the left down and keeping your torso straight.
- After 8 reps, switch sides.

TREADMILL PUSH
25 SECONDS

- Lean forward and hold the handles of a treadmill.
- With your feet toward the end of the treadmill, run while leaning toward the front of the treadmill, "pushing" forward with your feet.

MEDICINE BALL DOUBLE CRUNCH
15 REPS

- Lie on the floor holding a medicine ball over your head.
- Lift the ball up and lift your upper body off the ground while bending your knees and bring them up to meet the ball.
- Repeat for 1 rep.
- Keep the ball and your feet off the ground throughout.

BLOCK 3 (THREE CIRCUITS)

DEAD BALL EXPLOSIVE WALL THROW
3 REPS EACH SIDE

- Start down on your right knee, left foot on the ground, knee bent at 90 degrees.
- Position yourself about six feet from the wall.
- Push-up on your left leg and take one big step toward the wall with your right while throwing the ball off of it.
- After 3 reps, switch legs and repeat.

SHOULDER 30S
10 REPS EACH POSITION

- Stand straight with your arms at your sides and a dumbbell in each hand.
- Lift your arms straight up at your sides to slightly above shoulder height and back down twice for 1 rep (lateral).
- Lift your arms straight up in front, palms down, to shoulder height and back down twice for 1 rep (frontal).
- Bend your knees and bend forward at the waist, bend your elbows slightly and bring your arms back and forward twice for 1 rep (flies).

STABILITY BALL HAMSTRING CURLS
12 REPS

- Lie on the ground with your arms out to the sides, palms down on ground and feet up on a stability ball.
- Lift your hips so everything but your head and shoulders are off the ground.
- Roll the ball toward your butt with your feet.

STABILITY BALL PLANKS
25 SECONDS

- Put your elbows and forearms on a stability ball, palms facing up.
- Put your body in plank position and get up on your toes.
- Hold this position for the allotted time.

METABOLIC

BATTLE ROPES
THREE SETS OF 30 SECONDS

CHOOSE ONE OF THREE POSSIBILITIES

- Two-handed chops: Make chopping motions while holding the battle ropes, alternating your hands to make waves.

- Slams: Pick up and slam down the battle ropes with both hands.

- Wave lunges: Do two-handed chops while doing forward lunges.

FRIDAY

DAILY WARM-UP

- Refer to page 14.

MOVEMENT SERIES

SINGLE- AND DOUBLE-LEGGED HURDLES
3 REPS

- Place 5 mini hurdles 1 yard apart.
- Run through placing each foot between the hurdles. (See pictures on page 23.)
- Then run through placing both feet between the hurdles. (See pictures on page 47.)

L DRILL WITH CONES

- Place three cones in an L shape five yards apart.
- Run from cone A to cone B, touch the ground and run back to cone A.
- Run from cone A around the outside of cone B and make a figure eight around cone C.
- Sprint back around the outside of cone B to cone A.

ICKY SHUFFLE LADDERS

- Lay out a ladder on the ground. Go through the ladder touching your left foot to the outside of each opening, both feet inside (right-left) and then your right foot out on the right side before moving on to the next one.

CORE SERIES

PAD PUNCHES
15 REPS EACH POSITION

POSITION 1

- Get into a sit-up position and have your partner hold an Airex pad even with your left hip and at a height so the middle of the pad is about shoulder height at the top of a sit-up. Do a sit-up, turn left and hit the pad with an open right hand.

POSITION 2

- Have your partner move to your right side.
- Do a sit-up, turn right and hit the pad with an open left hand.

POSITION 3

- Have your partner stand at your feet.
- Do a sit-up and hit the pad with both open hands.

BLOCK 1 (THREE CIRCUITS)

BAND SQUAT
25 SECONDS

- Wrap two bands around stationary equipment at about foot height, then attach the other ends to either side of a barbell.
- Get under the barbell in traditional squat position and face away from the band.
- Bend at your knees and waist into a near sitting position and then straighten.
- Do as many as possible in the allotted time.

BIKE
25 SECONDS

- Bike as fast as possible for the allotted time.

BARBELL BAND BENCH
25 SECONDS

- Attach a band from the bottom of a bench to each side of a bar.
- Bench press, bringing the bar all the way down to your chest and back up as many times as possible in the allotted time.

BAND ROW
25 SECONDS

- Wrap a band around stationary equipment at about waist height.
- Hold the ends in both hands with your palms facing down.
- Bend at your knees and waist into a near sitting position that puts the band at chest height.
- Pull back, bending your elbows and turning your hands 90 degrees so your palms are facing each other.
- Pull all the way back until your hands are at your body and then straighten your arms again.
- Repeat for the allotted time.

BLOCK 2 (THREE CIRCUITS)

BAND SQUAT TO WRAP
25 SECONDS

- Wrap a band around stationary equipment at about knee height.
- Hold each end and face away from the band.
- Bend at your knees and waist into a near sitting position.
- Straighten your body and arms and bring them up and together, clapping in front of your face.
- Repeat for the allotted time.

BAND HIGH PULL
25 SECONDS

- Wrap a band around the base of a bench.
- Stand straight and hold both ends of the band with your palms facing down.
- Pull toward your face, bending your elbows straight out and finishing with your hands at your face and your arms bent and at a 90-degree angle from your body before straightening your arms again.
- Repeat for the allotted time.

BAND BI (BICEP CURLS WITH BAND)
25 SECONDS

- Wrap a TRX band around the base of a bench or another stationary object.
- Stand straight and hold each handle of the band with your palms down.
- Bend your elbows up into a biceps curl while turning your hands until your palms are up.
- Straighten your arms back down.
- Repeat for the allotted time.

BAND TRI
25 SECONDS

- Wrap a band around a pull-up bar.
- Grip the band at each end with palms facing down.
- Straighten your arms in a downward motion, then slowly lift up.
- Repeat for the allotted time.

BLOCK 3 (THREE CIRCUITS)

BATTLE ROPES
25 SECONDS

CHOOSE ONE OF THREE POSSIBILITIES

- Two-handed chops: Make chopping motions while holding the battle ropes, alternating your hands to make waves.

- Slams: Pick up and slam down the battle ropes with both hands.

- Wave lunges: Do two-handed chops while doing forward lunges.

V-UPS
25 SECONDS

- Lie on your back, legs straight and arms over your head. For more of a challenge, hold a weighted medicine ball.
- Bend at the waist, touch your fingers or the ball to your toes to make a V shape (you can bend your knees slightly).
- Return to the start position.
- Do as many as you can in the allotted time.

METABOLIC

BATTLE ROPES
THREE SETS OF 30 SECONDS

CHOOSE ONE OF THREE POSSIBILITIES

- Two-handed chops: Make chopping motions while holding the battle ropes, alternating your hands to make waves.

- Slams: Pick up and slam down the battle ropes with both hands.

- Wave lunges: Do two-handed chops while doing forward lunges.

WEEK 8

How was the week? Did you enjoy the new phase?

By now, you should be feeling strong, fast and powerful. You have done enough work to push you through to the end. This week, we will continue our speed phase and prepare ourselves for the final phase of football-specific routines.

Continue to focus on technique and be sure not to lose it just to speed up an exercise. If you have to slow things down in order to get it right, that is fine, just be sure to drop weight in order to keep the speed if you can't up the speed at that weight.

I'm proud of the work you've done up to this point. Let's keep it going!

Train hard!

MONDAY

DAILY WARM-UP

- Refer to page 14.

MOVEMENT SERIES

SUICIDE SHUFFLE

- Place markers 5 yards apart to 25 yards (you can use football field lines).
- Shuffle sideways to the first marker 5 yards awayand then sprint back to start.
- Shuffle sideways 10 yards and then sprint back to start.
- Shuffle sideways 15 yards and then sprint back to start.
- Shuffle sideways 20 yards and then sprint back to start.
- Shuffle sideways 25 yards and then sprint back to start.
- Do this once and then turn in the opposite direction and do it again.

CORE SERIES

PILLAR SERIES
25 SECONDS EACH POSITION

- Lie facedown on a bench with your waist at the end so your upper body is hanging over the edge, have a partner sit on your legs at your calves and hold yourself up even with the bench with your arms held to your side.
- With your partner still sitting on your legs at your calves, turn to the right, arms straight at your sides and hold yourself up even with the bench.
- With your partner still sitting on your legs at your calves, turn to the left, arms straight at your sides and hold yourself up even with the bench.
- Turn onto your back, have a partner sit on your legs at your shins, cross your arms across your chest and hold yourself up even with the bench.
- In all four parts of the series, make sure your body is straight and parallel to the ground, even with the bench.

BLOCK 1 (THREE CIRCUITS)

3-POSITION CLEAN
3 REPS

- Stand straight and hold a barbell with straight arms.
- Bend down a little until the barbell is at the top of your thigh.
- Jump slightly and bend your knees, waist and elbows, bringing the barbell up to your shoulders, gripping it so your palms are facing upward.
- Bring the barbell back down.
- Bend forward a little until the barbell is at the midpoint of your thigh.
- Jump slightly and bend your knees, waist and elbows, bringing the barbell up to your shoulders, gripping it so your palms are facing upward.
- Bring the barbell back down.
- Bend forward until the barbell is just below your knees.
- Jump slightly and bend your knees, waist and elbows, bringing the barbell up to your shoulders, gripping it so your palms are facing upward.
- Bring the barbell back down.

KETTLEBELL OFFSET FRONT SQUAT
8 REPS EACH SIDE

- Stand straight with your feet shoulder-width apart.
- Holding a kettlebell in your right hand, bend your right elbow completely and hold it at shoulder height perpendicular to your body.
- Hold your left arm straight out in front of you at shoulder height and bend your knees and waist into a sitting position.
- Stand back up.

BIKE
25 SECONDS

- Bike as fast as possible for the allotted time.

QUAD HIP FLEXOR STRETCH
6 REPS EACH SIDE

- Place your right knee bent on an Airex pad that is on the ground and rest the top of your right foot on a stability ball or bench so that the bottom of the foot is facing the ceiling. Your left leg should be in front in a bent position.
- Lean forward, bending your left knee forward and reaching your right arm diagonally into the air.

BLOCK 2 (THREE CIRCUITS)

INCLINE BENCH (135 POUNDS)
10 REPS

- Lie back on an incline bench with your feet flat on the floor. Bring a bar down to your chest and back up.

BAND PUSH-UP
20 REPS

- Put a band under your palms and around your back, across your shoulder blades. Do push-ups.

IPSILATERAL KETTLEBELL ROMANIAN DEAD LIFT
8 REPS

- Hold a kettlebell in your right hand. Bend at the waist and raise your left leg into the air behind you, keeping it straight. Touch the kettlebell to the ground and stand up.
- Switch and hold the kettlebell in your left hand. Bend at the waist and raise your right leg in the air behind you, keeping it straight. Touch the kettlebell to the ground and stand up.
- That is 1 rep.

LEG RAISES
15 REPS

- Hold on to a pull-up bar with a neutral grip and your arms toward the edges of the bar so your body makes a Y.
- Bend at the waist, pulling both legs up and out in front while keeping them together.

BLOCK 3 (THREE CIRCUITS)

BOX JUMP TWO TO ONE
3 REPS EACH SIDE

- Stand a couple of feet from a plyo box, facing it.
- Swing your arms over your head and down past your sides while bending your knees and forward at the waist.
- Jump off of both feet and land on the box on your right foot.
- Do 3 reps and then repeat landing on your left foot.

REACTIVE MEDICINE BALL WALL THROW
5 REPS EACH SIDE

- Stand a few feet from a wall, bent slightly forward with your right shoulder facing the wall.
- Hold a medicine ball at your waist.
- Jump away from the wall, landing on your left foot with your right leg bent and in the air behind you.
- Jump back toward the wall, landing on your right foot, throw the ball sideways off the wall and catch the rebound.

OBLIQUE BAND ROTATION
10 REPS EACH SIDE

- Attach a band to stationary equipment at mid-torso height.
- Grab the end with both hands with your left shoulder facing where the band is attached.
- With straight arms, turn your torso and hips as far as you can to the right.
- Return to the starting point.

FARMER'S WALK
50 YARDS

- With kettlebells in each hand and arms at your sides, walk forward.

METABOLIC

PARTNER PLANK
THREE SETS OF 30 SECONDS

- Get in the plank position with with your palms up (your elbows and forearms on an Airex pad if you like), legs slightly wider than shoulder-width apart and balanced on your toes.
- Have your partner get in the plank position facing you.
- Both of you lift your left arms, reach across and touch hands.
- Bring your left arms back down and then lift your right arms, reach across and touch hands.
- If you don't have a partner, place a dumbbell on its end and touch it with your hands when extending your arms.

TUESDAY

DAILY WARM-UP

- Refer to page 14.

MOVEMENT SERIES

SINGLE- AND DOUBLE-LEGGED HURDLES
3 REPS

- Place 5 mini hurdles 1 yard apart.
- Run through placing each foot between the hurdles. (See pictures on page 23.)
- Then run through placing both feet between the hurdles. (See pictures on page 47.)

L DRILL WITH CONES

- Place three cones in an L shape five yards apart.
- Run from cone A to cone B, touch the ground and run back to cone A.
- Run from cone A around the outside of cone B and make a figure eight around cone C.
- Sprint back around the outside of cone B to cone A.

ICKY SHUFFLE LADDERS

- Lay out a ladder on the ground. Go through the ladder touching your left foot to the outside of each opening, both feet inside (right–left) and then your right foot out on the right side before moving on to the next one.

CORE SERIES

PUSH-UP SCAPULAR PILLAR SERIES
25 SECONDS, 15 SECONDS EACH POSITION

- Hold your body at the top push-up position for 25 seconds. Lower yourself to the floor, then make a Y with your arms straight, lifting your head, chest, arms and feet off the ground (hold hand weights for a greater challenge). Hold for 15 seconds.

- Lower your body, then move to the midpoint of a push-up and hold for 25 seconds. Lower yourself, then make a T with your arms straight, lifting your head, chest, arms and feet off the ground (hold hand weights for a greater challenge). Hold for 15 seconds.

- Lower your body, then move to the lowest point of a push-up and hold for 25 seconds. Lower yourself, then make a W with your arms, bending your elbows so your hands are at ear level and lifting your head, chest, arms and feet off the ground (hold hand weights for a greater challenge). Hold for 15 seconds. Lower your body.

BLOCK 1 (THREE CIRCUITS)

SINGLE-ARM DUMBBELL SNATCH TO PRESS
4 REPS EACH ARM

- Stand with your feet shoulder-width apart and a dumbbell horizontally between them.
- Bend down and grab the dumbbell with your right hand.
- In one motion, jump and lift the dumbbell over your head.
- Bend your elbow, bringing the dumbbell to your shoulder and then press it over your head, straightening your arm.
- Bend at the waist until the dumbbell touches the floor.

CONTRALATERAL ROW
8 REPS EACH SIDE

- Hold a dumbbell or powerblock in your right hand.
- Bend forward at your waist, lifting your straight right leg back until it's parallel with the ground. Your left leg can be slightly bent.
- Bend your right elbow, raising the dumbbell to your body, and then straighten.

SINGLE-ARM ALTERNATING KETTLEBELL SWING
8 REPS

- Stand straight with your feet shoulder-width apart.
- Hold a kettlebell in your right hand.
- Bending your knees, swing the kettlebell back between your legs, then up with a straight arm to shoulder height and switch hands at the top height.
- With the kettlebell in your left hand, swing it back between your legs and up high where you switch hands again.

BAND JUMP
5 REPS

- Attach one band to each side of the bottom of a barbell rack.
- Turn with your back toward the rack.
- Take the band from the right side, put the loop over your head and down on your left shoulder.
- Take the band from the left side, put the loop over your head and down on your right shoulder.
- Swing your arms up in front of your body, over your head with bent arms and then bring them down, bending your knees, and push off and jump.

BLOCK 2 (THREE CIRCUITS)

REAR FOOT ELEVATED BARBELL BAND SPLIT SQUAT
5 REPS EACH SIDE

- Bend your right leg at the knee and put your right toes on the middle of a plyo box.
- Attach bands from the floor to the outside of a bar.
- With the bar resting across your back below the neck and your left foot slightly in front of your body, bend your left knee, dipping your right knee down and then lift up.

QUAD HIP FLEXOR STRETCH
6 REPS BOTH SIDES

- Place your right knee bent on an Airex pad that is on the ground and rest the top of your right foot on a stability ball or bench so that the bottom of the foot is facing the ceiling. Your left leg should be in front in a bent position.
- Lean forward, bending your left knee forward and reaching your right arm diagonally into the air.

IPSILATERAL KETTLEBELL ROW
8 REPS EACH SIDE

- Hold a kettlebell or dumbbell in your right hand. Bend at the waist and raise your right leg into the air behind you, keeping it straight.
- Bend your right arm at the elbow, raise it as far as you can, straighten it and lower the kettlebell to the ground.
- After 8 reps, switch legs and repeat with the kettlebell in your left hand.

FACE PULL
15 REPS

- Attach a band to the top of a jungle gym so it's coming down at a 45-degree angle.
- Bend your knees and waist as if you're sitting down halfway.
- Bend your elbows, pull back the band toward your face and then straighten your arms.

BLOCK 3 (THREE CIRCUITS)

DUMBBELL PUSH-UP TO ROW
5 REPS

- Get in push-up position with your hands on the dumbbells.
- Do a full push-up, down and up.
- Bend your right arm up until the dumbbell is even with your ribs.
- Straighten your arm back down to the ground.
- Bend your left arm up until the dumbbell is even with your ribs.
- Straighten your arm back to the ground.

BAND ROW
25 SECONDS

- Wrap a band around stationary equipment at about waist height.
- Hold the ends in both hands with your palms facing down.
- Bend at your knees and waist into a near sitting position that puts the band at chest height.
- Pull back, bending your elbows and turning your hands 90 degrees so your palms are facing each other.
- Pull all the way back until your hands are at your body and then straighten your arms again.
- Repeat for the allotted time.

MEDICINE BALL PARALLEL WALL THROW
10 REPS

- Stand a few feet from a wall and face the wall holding a medicine ball in both hands at your waist.
- Bend your knees and waist, holding the ball in both hands and swinging it around to your right side. Throw it against the wall and catch it.
- Bend your knees and waist, swing the ball to your left side with both arms. Throw it against the wall and catch it.

PLANK WALKS
25 YARDS

- Put Valslides under the toes of both feet and get in push-up position.
- Walk forward with your hands, allowing your feet to just slide behind.

METABOLIC

INCLINE BAND FLIES
THREE SETS OF 30 SECONDS

- Wrap a band underneath the base of an incline bench, lie back on it and hold an end in each hand with your arms extended to the sides at chest height.
- Keeping your arms straight, bring your hands together then back out to the side.
- Do as many as possible in 30 seconds.

WEDNESDAY

DAILY WARM-UP

- Refer to page 14.

RECOVERY

- Use a foam roller to go over all your soft tissue.

THURSDAY

DAILY WARM-UP

- Refer to page 14.

MOVEMENT SERIES

SUICIDE SHUFFLE

- Place markers 5 yards apart to 25 yards (you can use football field lines).
- Shuffle sideways to the first marker 5 yards away and then sprint back to start.
- Shuffle sideways 10 yards and then sprint back to start.
- Shuffle sideways 15 yards and then sprint back to start.
- Shuffle sideways 20 yards and then sprint back to start.
- Shuffle sideways 25 yards and then sprint back to start.
- Do this once and then turn in the opposite direction and do it again.

CORE SERIES

SEATED MEDICINE BALL THROWS
THREE SETS OF 15 REPS

- From a seated position on the floor, throw a medicine ball back and forth with a partner two to three yards away.
- If there is no partner available, throw the ball against the wall.

BLOCK 1 (THREE CIRCUITS)

DUMBBELL SQUAT TO JUMP TO FORWARD LUNGE
5 REPS EACH LEG

- Stand straight with your legs shoulder-width apart.
- With a dumbbell in each hand, bend your knees and waist into a sitting position.
- Stand back up and jump.
- Step forward with your right leg, bend your right knee and dip your left knee toward the ground.
- Step back to the starting position.

ERIC WINSTON

Offensive Tackle
#73 Cincinnati Bengals
6-7, 302 pounds
Past teams: Houston Texans, Kansas City Chiefs, Arizona Cardinals

I came to Nine Innovations because I wanted to go somewhere that would push me to be a better athlete and that would take a smart approach to training. The biggest benefit I have seen is in core strength, joint stability, flexibility and quickness.

Abdul and Nine Innovations have helped extend my career with its innovative approach through stressing core strength and flexibility. Furthermore, Nine Innovations doesn't subscribe to "traditional" lifting circuits. Instead, Abdul and his staff come up with specific training that meets the needs that I have.

DUMBBELL REVERSE LUNGE TO KNEE DRIVE
8 REPS EACH SIDE

- Stand straight with your legs close together, a dumbbell in each hand.
- Step back with your left leg, bending your right knee to 90 degrees and your left knee until it's nearly touching the ground.
- Lift your left foot and bring your leg forward, past the center and lift up your bent left knee as high as you can.

QUAD HIP FLEXOR STRETCH
6 REPS EACH SIDE

- Place your right knee bent on an Airex pad that is on the ground and rest the top of your right foot on a stability ball or bench so that the bottom of the foot is facing the ceiling. Your left leg should be in front in a bent position.
- Lean forward, bending your left knee forward and reaching your right arm diagonally into the air.

RESISTED RUN
25 SECONDS

- Wrap a band around your waist and around a stationary object on the floor.
- Lean forward slightly and run for the allotted time.

BLOCK 2 (THREE CIRCUITS)

BARBELL BAND JUMP SQUAT
5 REPS

- Attach bands from the bottom of the bench to each side of a bar.
- With your feet shoulder-width apart and your hands positioned a little wider than your feet, rest the bar on the back of your neck.
- Stand straight and then squat and jump. Squat and jump for specified number of reps.

MEDICINE BALL SQUAT WALL THROW
5 REPS

- Stand a few feet from the wall and hold a medicine ball at your chest.
- Squat, then push up on your toes and throw the ball high off the wall. Let it hit the ground and then pick it up to throw again.

INCLINE DUMBBELL ROW
8 REPS

- Lie on your stomach on a bench inclined about 45 degrees.
- Hold the dumbbells with your arms straight down, then bend your elbows, pulling the weights up to your body and then lowering them back down.

BODY SAW
10 REPS

- Place your feet on Valslides and your elbows on an Airex pad with your body fully extended and held parallel to the ground. Your elbows should be bent at a 90-degree angle, holding your body up, and your palms should be facing up.
- Without moving your elbows, use your arms to push your body back and then pull it forward.

BLOCK 3 (THREE CIRCUITS)

LATERAL ROTATION BOX JUMPS
3 REPS EACH SIDE

- Stand about a foot from a plyo box with your legs shoulder-width apart.
- Raise your arms over your head, swing them down, bend your knees and bend forward at the waist.
- Swing your arms up and jump onto the box while turning 90 degrees so that you land facing to the right.

DEAD BALL SQUAT TO WALL THROW
5 REPS

- Hold a dead ball at your chest with your elbows bent and legs shoulder-width apart.
- Squat, bending at your knees and waist, and then come up and throw the dead ball against the wall.

WIDE-LEGGED SEATED KETTLEBELL ROTATIONAL PRESS
8 REPS

- Sit with your legs spread into a wide V in front of you.
- Hold a kettlebell in each hand at shoulder height with bent elbows.
- Straighten your right arm up and out, in front of your head on a diagonal.
- Bring it down and repeat with the opposite arm.

VALSLIDE PIKES
15 REPS

- Put Valslides under each foot and get in push-up position.
- Slide feet up together as far as you can then back down.

METABOLIC

BAND BI (BICEP CURLS WITH BAND)
THREE SETS OF 30 SECONDS

- Wrap a TRX band around the base of a bench or another stationary object.
- Stand straight and hold each handle of the band with your palms down.
- Bend your elbows up into a biceps curl while turning your hands until your palms are up.
- Straighten your arms back down.
- Repeat for the allotted time.

FRIDAY

DAILY WARM-UP

- Refer to page 14.

MOVEMENT SERIES

SINGLE- AND DOUBLE-LEGGED HURDLES
3 REPS

- Place 5 mini hurdles 1 yard apart.
- Run through placing each foot between the hurdles. (See pictures on page 23.)
- Then run through placing both feet between the hurdles. (See pictures on page 47.)

L DRILL WITH CONES

- Place three cones in an *L* shape five yards apart.
- Run from cone A to cone B, touch the ground and run back to cone A.
- Run from cone A around the outside of cone B and make a figure eight around cone C.
- Sprint back around the outside of cone B to cone A.

ICKY SHUFFLE LADDERS

- Lay out ladder on the ground. Go through ladder—touching left foot to the outside of each opening, both feet inside (right-left) then right foot out on the right side before moving on to the next one.

CORE SERIES

PAD PUNCHES
15 REPS EACH POSITION

POSITION 1

- Get into a sit-up position and have your partner hold an Airex pad even with your left hip and at a height so the middle of the pad is about shoulder height at the top of a sit-up. Do a sit-up, turn left and hit the pad with an open right hand.

POSITION 2

- Have your partner move to your right side.
- Do a sit-up, turn right and hit the pad with an open left hand.

POSITION 3

- Have your partner stand at your feet.
- Do a sit-up and hit the pad with both open hands.

BLOCK 1 (THREE CIRCUITS)

SNATCH GRIP HIGH PULL
5 REPS

- Stand straight with your legs slightly more than shoulder-width apart.
- Hold a barbell with your palms down and your hands about six inches wider than your hips.
- Bend forward at the waist and slightly at the knees, bend your elbows and quickly pull the barbell up to your chest and back down.

JUNGLE GYM WEIGHTED ROW
10 REPS

- In this exercise, your body is going to be parallel to the ground, elevated at bench level.
- Hang a TRX band so the handles are a foot above a bench or plyo box.
- Hold the handles and put your feet up on the bench or box, toes pointed toward the ceiling.
- Have a partner put a plate on your chest.
- Bend your arms and pull your straight body up to the band handles and lower yourself back down.

SNATCH GRIP ABS
15 REPS

- Get in sit-up start position and hold a barbell over your chest.
- Do a sit-up, hold the barbell over your head at the height of the sit-up.
- Come back down, holding the bar with straight arms and finishing with your back on the ground and the bar again above your chest.

PRETZEL STRETCH
6 REPS EACH SIDE

- Lie on the ground on your left side. With your right arm, grab your left ankle from behind you.
- Rest your right knee in front of you on the ground perpendicular with your torso.
- Hold your right knee to the ground with your left hand.
- Drive your right shoulder parallel to the ground behind you.

BLOCK 2 (THREE CIRCUITS)

VALSLIDE LUNGE
6 REPS

- Stand straight with your right foot on an Airex pad and a Valslide under your left foot.
- Slide your left leg back, bending your right knee and lifting your arms up until your hands are in front of your face.
- When your left foot gets near to the farthest point, bend your left knee until it is just off the ground and then slide back to stand straight.

INCLINE BAND BENCH
8 REPS

- Attach a band from the bottom of a bench to each side of a bar.
- With the bench inclined, bench press, bringing the bar all the way down to your chest and back up.

ECCENTRIC NEUTRAL GRIP PULL-UPS
5 REPS

- Grip the bars that are perpendicular to the pull-up bar with your palms facing each other.
- Pull up until your head is over the bar and then take five seconds to lower yourself.

BATTLE ROPES
25 SECONDS

CHOOSE ONE OF THREE POSSIBILITIES

- Two-handed chops: Make chopping motions while holding the battle ropes, alternating your hands to make waves.

- Slams: Pick up and slam down the battle ropes with both hands.

- Wave lunges: Do two-handed chops while doing forward lunges.

BLOCK 3 (THREE CIRCUITS)

MEDICINE BALL CHEST PASS
25 SECONDS

- Hold a medicine ball at your chest, push and throw it to a partner. If you don't have a partner, throw the ball into a wall.

JUNGLE GYM (OR TRX BAND) REVERSE FLIES
10 REPS

- With TRX bands hanging down from the top of equipment, grab a handle with each hand and lean all the way back until you're balancing on your heels.
- Keep your arms straight and the handles even with your shoulders.
- Pull up and push your arms out into a fly, keeping your toes off the ground.
- Lower back down.

MEDICINE BALL PERPENDICULAR WALL THROW
10 REPS EACH SIDE

- Stand perpendicular to the wall, your left shoulder nearest it about two feet away.
- Hold a ball about stomach height.
- Bend at your knees and twist to the right, away from the wall.
- When turning back to the wall, throw the ball at it and catch the rebound.

KETTLEBELL SIT-UP TO ROTATIONAL PRESS
8 REPS

- Get in the sit-up start position with a kettlebell in each hand and your elbows bent so the kettlebells are at your shoulders.
- Do a sit-up and at the height of the sit-up extend your right arm diagonally up and across in front of your face and then bring it down.
- Extend your left arm and do the same.
- Lower yourself back to the start position.

BATTLE ROPES
THREE SETS OF 30 SECONDS

CHOOSE ONE OF THREE POSSIBILITIES

- Two-handed chops: Make chopping motions while holding the battle ropes, alternating your hands to make waves.

- Slams: Pick up and slam down the battle ropes with both hands.

- Wave lunges: Do two-handed chops while doing forward lunges.

WEEK 9

We're at the last week of the speed phase! You are well on your way to becoming a great football player.

Remember, this program is not easy, and those who choose to do what others won't will reap the benefits.

This week, let's finish strong with speed and increase the weight so we can hit that max power phase.

We're introducing four circuits into the workout. It's going to be tough but worth it!

Again, really concentrate on technique, and if you have any minor aches or pains, be sure to take Wednesday off to nurse those ailments.

Keep it up! Train hard!

MONDAY

DAILY WARM-UP

Refer to page 14.

MOVEMENT SERIES

SUICIDE SHUFFLE

- Place markers 5 yards apart to 25 yards (you can use football field lines).
- Shuffle sideways to the first marker 5 yards away and then sprint back to start.
- Shuffle sideways 10 yards and then sprint back to start.
- Shuffle sideways 15 yards and then sprint back to start.
- Shuffle sideways 20 yards and then sprint back to start.
- Shuffle sideways 25 yards and then sprint back to start.
- Do this once and then turn in the opposite direction and do it again.

CORE SERIES

PILLAR SERIES
30 SECONDS EACH POSITION

- Lie facedown on a bench with your waist at the end so your upper body is hanging over the edge, have a partner sit on your legs at your calves and hold yourself up even with the bench with your arms held to your side.
- With your partner still sitting on your legs at your calves, turn to the right, arms straight at your sides and hold yourself up even with the bench.
- With your partner still sitting on your legs at your calves, turn to the left, arms straight at your sides and hold yourself up even with the bench.
- Turn onto your back, have a partner sit on your legs at your shins, cross your arms across your chest and hold yourself up even with the bench.
- In all four parts of the series, make sure your body is straight and parallel to the ground, even with the bench.

BLOCK 1 (FOUR CIRCUITS)

DUMBBELL CLEAN TO ARMPIT
8 REPS

- Stand with your feet shoulder-width apart.
- Bend your knees and waist and hold a dumbbell in each hand at your knees.
- Bend your elbows, pulling the dumbbells up toward your armpits and lifting yourself onto your toes.
- Finish by standing straight and then get back into starting position.

CONTRALATERAL VALSLIDE LUNGE
8 REPS EACH LEG (FIRST CIRCUIT), 6 REPS (SECOND), 5 REPS (THIRD), 4 REPS (FOURTH)

- Stand straight with your legs together and a Valslide under your left foot.
- Hold a kettlebell or powerblock (show in photos) in your left hand and keep your arms straight down at your sides.
- Slide your left leg back, bending your right knee and dipping your left knee toward the floor, then straighten to the start position.

QUAD HIP FLEXOR STRETCH
6 REPS EACH SIDE

- Place your right knee bent on an Airex pad that is on the ground and rest the top of your right foot on a stability ball or bench so that the bottom of the foot is facing the ceiling. Your left leg should be in front in a bent position.
- Lean forward, bending your left knee forward and reaching your right arm diagonally into the air.

ALTERNATE DUMBBELL BENCH
8 REPS EACH ARM

- Lie on your back on a bench with your knees bent at the end and your feet flat on the ground.
- Hold the dumbbells with your elbows bent and the dumbbells at your side, palms pointing upward.
- Straighten your right arm all the way up, and then bring it all the way back down.
- Then straighten your left arm and bring it back down.

BLOCK 2 (THREE CIRCUITS)

DUMBBELL PUSH-UP TO ROW
8 REPS

- Get in push-up position with your hands on the dumbbells.
- Do a full push-up, down and up.
- Bend your right arm up until the dumbbell is even with your ribs.
- Straighten your arm back down to the ground.
- Bend your left arm up until the dumbbell is even with your ribs.
- Straighten your arm back to the ground.

MEDICINE BALL WALL CHEST THROWS
30 SECONDS

- Stand arm distance from the wall with your knees and waist slightly bent.
- Hold a medicine ball with your arms fully extended.
- Bring the ball to your chest, throw it into the wall and catch it when it bounces back.

SLED SPRINT
MAXIMUM 25 YARDS, 2 REPS

- Push a sled as fast as possible.

PLANK WITH ROTATION
8 REPS

- Get in the plank position with your arms elevated on an Airex pad and turned so your forearms are perpendicular to your body.
- Lift your left arm up and rotate your body, straightening your arm so it ends up with your fingers pointing toward the ceiling.
- Bring your arm back down and repeat with your right arm.

BLOCK 3 (THREE CIRCUITS)

JUNGLE GYM (OR TRX) SINGLE-LEGGED HAMSTRING CURLS
5 REPS EACH SIDE

- Put your feet in the TRX handles hanging on a jungle gym about six inches off the ground.
- Lie on your back with straight arms out from your sides and palms down on the floor.
- Bend your right knee all the way, bringing your feet up toward your butt.
- Straighten.

SHOULDER 30S
10 REPS EACH POSITION

- Stand straight with your arms at your sides and a dumbbell in each hand.
- Lift your arms straight up at your sides to slightly above shoulder height and back down twice for 1 rep (lateral).
- Lift your arms straight up in front, palms down, to shoulder height and back down twice for 1 rep (frontal).
- Bend your knees and bend forward at the waist, bend your elbows slightly and bring your arms back and forward twice for 1 rep (flies).

WIDE-LEGGED SEATED KETTLEBELL ROTATIONAL PRESS
8 REPS

- Sit with your legs spread into a wide V in front of you.
- Hold a kettlebell in each hand at shoulder height with bent elbows.
- Straighten your right arm up and out, in front of your head on a diagonal.
- Bring it down and repeat with the opposite arm.

X PULL DOWN
12 REPS

- Attach bands to a pull-up bar, cross them and hold the ends.
- Stand facing a jungle gym with your feet shoulder-width apart.
- Straighten your arms, pulling all the way back behind your body, then bend your elbows and return to the starting position.

METABOLIC

INCLINE BAND FLIES
THREE SETS OF 40 SECONDS

- Wrap a band underneath the base of an incline bench, lie on it and hold an end in each hand with your arms extended to the sides at chest height.
- Keeping your arms straight, bring your hands together then back out to the side.
- Do as many as possible in the allotted time.

TUESDAY

DAILY WARM-UP

- Refer to page 14.

MOVEMENT SERIES

SLED SPRINT
50 YARDS

- Push a sled as fast as possible for 50 yards.

L DRILL WITH CONES

- Place three cones in an *L* shape five yards apart.
- Run from cone A to cone B and back.
- Run from cone A around the outside of cone B and make a figure eight around cone C.
- Sprint back around the outside of cone B to cone A.

LATERAL SINGLE-LEGGED LADDERS

- Lay a ladder out on the ground. Stand to the side of the ladder, face it and run, placing each foot in each space between the rungs and bringing it back outside the ladder, moving from one end to the other.

CORE SERIES

PUSH-UP SCAPULAR PILLAR SERIES
30 SECONDS, 20 SECONDS EACH POSITION

- Hold your body at the top push-up position for 30 seconds. Lower yourself to the floor, then make a Y with your arms straight, lifting your head, chest, arms and feet off the ground (hold hand weights for a greater challenge). Hold for 20 seconds.
- Lower your body, then move to the midpoint of a push-up and hold for 30 seconds. Lower yourself, then make a T with your arms straight, lifting your head, chest, arms and feet off the ground (hold hand weights for a greater challenge). Hold for 20 seconds.
- Lower your body, then move to the lowest point of a push-up and hold for 30 seconds. Lower yourself, then make a W with your arms, bending your elbows so your hands are at ear level and lifting your head, chest, arms and feet off the ground (hold hand weights for a greater challenge). Hold for 20 seconds. Lower your body.

BLOCK 1 (FOUR CIRCUITS)

SINGLE-LEGGED BARBELL RDL TO POWER SHRUG
8 REPS ON EACH LEG

- Stand straight with your legs together, holding a barbell just below your waist.
- Keeping both legs straight, lift your left leg behind you while bending at the waist and lowering the bar to the floor.
- Straighten, returning your left leg to the floor.
- Shrug your shoulders.

GLUTE ACTIVATION
10 REPS EACH SIDE, THEN 10 WITH BOTH LEGS TOGETHER

- Wrap mini bands around your knees and ankles, and get down in a squat position without letting your knees go past your toes.
- Turn your right knee out, pushing against the band's resistance. Turn your right knee back in, then turn out your left knee. Finally, turn both knees out together.

BARBELL STEP-UP
8 REPS EACH SIDE (FIRST CIRCUIT), 6 REPS (SECOND), 5 REPS (THIRD), 4 REPS (FOURTH)

- Hold a barbell on your shoulders behind your neck.
- Step up on a plyo box with your right leg, bend and bring up your left knee, and then step down with your left leg.
- Repeat stepping up with your left leg and bringing your right knee into the air.

BAND QUAD HIP FLEXOR STRETCH
6 REPS EACH LEG

- Kneel your right knee on a pad about three feet from stationary equipment.
- Bend your left knee and keep your left foot flat on floor.
- Attach a band from the stationary equipment to your right leg, wrapping it just above your hamstring.
- Bend your left knee and hips forward while straightening your right arm at about shoulder height.

BLOCK 2 (THREE CIRCUITS)

ECCENTRIC NEUTRAL GRIP PULL-UPS
8 REPS

- Grip the bars that are perpendicular to the pull-up bar with your palms facing each other.
- Pull up until your head is over the bar and then take 5 seconds to lower yourself.

PARTNER BAND ROW
8 REPS EACH ARM

- With a partner holding the other side of the band and your elbows bent, pull back one arm at a time to row.
- If you don't have a partner, attach the band to stationary equipment.

LATERAL STRETCH
6 REPS

- Stand with your legs shoulder-width apart.
- Put your right arm on your hip, left arm over your head and bend your body to the right.
- Switch arms and bend your body to the left.

REVERSE MEDICINE BALL WALL THROW
6 REPS

- Stand about two feet from a wall, facing away from the wall.
- Hold a medicine ball at your waist.
- Twist to the left, throw the ball off the wall and catch the rebound.
- Twist around to the right, throw the ball off the wall and catch the rebound.

BLOCK 3 (THREE CIRCUITS)

SINGLE-LEGGED SQUAT
8 REPS EACH LEG

- Stand with one foot on a plyo box and the other foot suspended in the air, and hold small counter weights in your hand.
- Squat slowly on the leg that is on the box. Use the counter weights to extend your arms in front of you.
- Go as low as you can and then straighten up.

DUMBBELL SLIDE REACH TO ROW
5 REPS EACH ARM

- Place a Valslide under a dumbbell.
- Get in push-up position with your left hand holding the dumbbell.
- Go down for a push-up and slide your straight left arm forward while bending the right.
- Come up, sliding your left arm back to the start position.
- Bend your left elbow, pulling the dumbbell up to your body and putting it back down.

DUMBBELL WOOD CHOP
8 REPS EACH SIDE

- Stand with your legs shoulder-width apart and your knees bent.
- With both hands holding a dumbbell, rotate your hips, turn to the right and bring the dumbbell up and above your right shoulder, bending your elbows slightly.
- Rotate back to the left and bring the dumbbell diagonally down toward your left knee.

BARBELL CURL 1½
10 REPS

- Stand straight with your feet shoulder-width apart.
- Hold a barbell with your arms straight and palms up.
- Curl, bringing the barbell to your shoulders.
- Straighten your arms, bring the barbell back up halfway and then straighten to the start position.

METABOLIC

BAND PULL DOWN
THREE SETS OF 40 SECONDS

- Sit on a bench with your back straight and one band attached to the top of each side of stationary equipment.
- Hold one band in each hand and bend your elbows, pulling down and then straighten your arms back up.

WEDNESDAY

DAILY WARM-UP

- Refer to page 14.

RECOVERY

- Use a foam roller to go over all your soft tissue.

THURSDAY

DAILY WARM-UP

- Refer to page 14.

MOVEMENT SERIES

SUICIDE SHUFFLE

- Place markers 5 yards apart to 25 yards (you can use football field lines).
- Shuffle sideways to the first marker 5 yards away and then sprint back to start.
- Shuffle sideways 10 yards and then sprint back to start.
- Shuffle sideways 15 yards and then sprint back to start.
- Shuffle sideways 20 yards and then sprint back to start.
- Shuffle sideways 25 yards and then sprint back to start.
- Do this once and then turn in the opposite direction and do it again.

CORE SERIES

SEATED MEDICINE BALL THROWS
THREE SETS OF 20 REPS

- From a seated position on the floor, throw a medicine ball back and forth with a partner two to three yards away.
- If there is no partner available, throw the ball against the wall.

BLOCK 1 (FOUR CIRCUITS)

SINGLE-ARM DUMBBELL SNATCH
5 REPS EACH ARM

- Standing straight, position your legs shoulder-width apart.
- Hold a dumbbell in your right hand with your arm straight out at shoulder height.
- Slightly bend at the waist and knees, lowering your straight arm until the dumbbell is between your legs and about even with your knees.
- In one motion, jump and lift your straight arm over your head.

INCLINE BENCH
10 REPS (FIRST CIRCUIT), 8 REPS (SECOND), 6 REPS (THIRD), 4 REPS (FOURTH)

- Lie back on an incline bench with your feet flat on the floor. Bring a bar down to your chest and back up.

PLATE PUSH-UP
10 REPS

- Set two barbell plates just outside of your hands.
- Do a push-up. When you come up, push to lift yourself off the ground, move your arms out and land with your hands on the plates.
- Do another push-up and lift yourself off the ground, moving your hands back to their original position.

JONATHAN GRIMES

Running Back
#41 Houston Texans
5-10, 209 pounds
Past teams: New York Jets, Jacksonville Jaguars

I chose to go to Nine Innovations so I could train with the high caliber athletes who were already training there. I feel like I have an edge on a lot of my opponents, because Abdul's workouts push me to different levels of strength and endurance, while also being smart and critically paying attention to how my body is responding to the workouts.

I have been able to stay exceptionally healthy throughout my seasons after training at Nine Innovations. The program helps me gauge what's going on with my body and I can be proactive with different issues that may come up during the season.

I would definitely recommend this program not only for all athletes, but anyone who wishes to improve their physical health. Workouts can be tailored to accommodate any particular needs relating to improving performance, flexibility, endurance and strength.

HEAVY WEIGHTED ABS
15 REPS (START AT 35 POUNDS AND GO UP AS NEEDED)

- Get in sit-up position with your arms bent holding a dumbbell or powerblock on your chest even with your shoulders.
- Do a sit-up, touching your elbows to your thighs and then going back down.

BLOCK 2 (THREE CIRCUITS)

WALKING LUNGE WITH ROTATION
8 REPS

- Hold a medicine ball at your waist.
- Step forward with your right leg, bending your knee to 90 degrees and dipping your left knee down.
- Rotate your torso to the right and back to center.
- Step forward with your left leg, bending your knee to 90 degrees and dipping your right knee down.
- Rotate your torso to the left and back to center.
- That is 1 rep.

QUAD HIP FLEXOR STRETCH
6 REPS EACH SIDE

- Place your right knee bent on an Airex pad that is on the ground and rest the top of your right foot on a stability ball or bench so that the bottom of the foot is facing the ceiling. Your left leg should be in front in a bent position.
- Lean forward, bending your left knee forward and reaching your right arm diagonally into the air.

BIKE
40 SECONDS

- Bike as fast as possible for the allotted time.

BATTLE ROPES
30 SECONDS

CHOOSE ONE OF THREE POSSIBILITIES

- Two-handed chops: Make chopping motions while holding the battle ropes, alternating your hands to make waves.

- Slams: Pick up and slam down the battle ropes with both hands.

- Wave lunges: Do two-handed chops while doing forward lunges.

BLOCK 3 (THREE CIRCUITS)

ROTATIONAL LIFT
8 REPS EACH SIDE

- Attach a band to a fixed object at the floor and hold it in both hands with your arms straight. Stand with your right shoulder closest to where the band is attached, then step your right leg back and lower into lunge position.
- Keeping your arms straight, lift them diagonally up and to the left, then lower them back down.

SPLIT-STANCE MEDICINE BALL OVERHEAD SLAMS
30 SECONDS

- With your right leg forward, knee bent at 90 degrees, and your left leg back balanced on your toes in the lunge position, hold a medicine ball at your waist, then bring it around to the left, swing it over your head while holding the ball with both hands and come down and slam the ball off the ground.
- Catch the ball on the bounce and swing it over your head to the right, bouncing it off the ground and catching it again.

DUMBBELL CHEST FLY
12 REPS

- Stand straight and hold a dumbbell in each hand with your arms extended to the sides at chest height.
- Keeping your arms straight, bring your hands together and then back out to the sides.

DUMBBELL SHOULDER SHRUG
12 REPS

- Hold a dumbbell in each hand, arms down at your sides, and shrug your shoulders.

METABOLIC

SUPINE BICEP CURLS
THREE SETS OF 40 SECONDS

- Lie on your back on the floor.
- Attach a band to a dumbbell at your feet (you can also wrap the band around your feet).
- Hold the band and do as many bicep curls as you can in the allotted time.

FRIDAY

DAILY WARM-UP

- Refer to page 14.

MOVEMENT SERIES

SLED SPRINT
50 YARDS

- Push a sled as fast as you can for 50 yards.

L DRILL WITH CONES
- Place three cones in an L shape five yards apart.
- Run from cone A to cone B and back.
- Run from cone A around the outside of cone B and make a figure eight around cone C.
- Sprint back around the outside of cone B to cone A.

LATERAL SINGLE-LEGGED LADDERS
- Lay a ladder out on the ground. Stand to the side of the ladder, face it and run, placing each foot in each space between the rungs and bringing it back outside the ladder, moving from one end to the other.

CORE SERIES

PAD PUNCHES
20 REPS EACH POSITION

POSITION 1

- Get into a sit-up position and have your partner hold an Airex pad even with your left hip and at a height so the middle of the pad is about shoulder height at the top of a sit-up. Do a sit-up, turn left and hit the pad with an open right hand.

POSITION 2

- Have your partner move to your right side.
- Do a sit-up, turn right and hit the pad with an open left hand.

POSITION 3

- Have your partner stand at your feet.
- Do a sit-up and hit the pad with both open hands.

BLOCK 1 (FOUR CIRCUITS)

BARBELL HIGH PULL/CLEAN/FRONT SQUAT
3 REPS EACH SIDE

- Stand straight with your legs shoulder-width apart.
- Hold a bar with your palms facing your body.
- Bend your elbows and bring the bar up to your chest and then straight back down.
- Bend your elbows and flip up so your palms are facing up and the bar is up to your shoulders and then straighten back down.
- Then do a front squat.

REAR FOOT ELEVATED BARBELL SPLIT SQUAT
8 REPS (FIRST CIRCUIT), 6 REPS (SECOND), 4 REPS (THIRD), 3 REPS (FOURTH)

- Bend your right leg at the knee and put your right toes on the middle of a plyo box.
- Attach bands from the floor to the outside of a bar.
- With the bar resting across your back below the neck and your left foot slightly in front of your body, bend your left knee, dipping your right knee down and then lift up.

SUMO SQUAT TO HAMSTRING STRETCH
6 REPS

- Bend at your knees and waist until you can grab your toes with both hands.
- Bend your knees farther and lower your butt toward the ground.
- Straighten your legs while still holding your toes.

JUNGLE GYM (OR TRX) MARCHES
10 REPS

- Hold the handles of TRX bands that are hanging from a jungle gym at about chest height.
- Lean forward, keeping your arms straight.
- Bend your left knee up and then straighten it back down.
- Bend your right knee up and then straighten it back down.

BLOCK 2 (THREE CIRCUITS)

CONTRALATERAL ROW
8 REPS EACH SIDE

- Hold a dumbbell or powerblock in your right hand.
- Bend forward at your waist, lifting your straight right leg back until it's parallel with the ground. Your left leg can be slightly bent.
- Bend your right elbow, raising the dumbbell to your body, and then straighten.

STICK STRETCH
6 REPS EACH SIDE

- Stand with your legs wider than shoulder-width.
- Have a stick about an arm's length from your body and hold it at shoulder height in your right hand.
- Bend your knees and waist until your torso is nearly parallel to the ground while still holding the stick.
- Pulse (small bounces) at shoulder/trap at the lowest point of the squat and then stand back up.

LATERAL BOX JUMP
5 REPS

- Stand to the left of a plyo box with your legs straight and slightly less than shoulder-width apart and your hands together at your chest.
- Bend your knees and jump sideways onto the box with both feet.
- Bend your knees and jump down to the other side of the box.
- Repeat the other way.
- That is 1 rep.

MEDICINE BALL PERPENDICULAR WALL THROW
10 REPS EACH SIDE

- Stand perpendicular to the wall, your left shoulder nearest it about two feet away.
- Hold a ball about stomach height.
- Bend at your knees and twist to the right, away from the wall.
- When turning back to the wall, throw the ball at it and catch the rebound.

BLOCK 3 (THREE CIRCUITS)

TREADMILL PUSH
30 SECONDS

- Lean forward and hold the handles of a treadmill.
- With your feet toward the end of the treadmill, run while leaning toward the front of the treadmill, "pushing" forward with your feet.

DUMBBELL WOOD CHOP
8 REPS EACH SIDE

- Stand with your legs shoulder-width apart and your knees bent.
- With both hands holding a dumbbell, rotate your hips, turn to the right and bring the dumbbell up and above your right shoulder, bending your elbows slightly.
- Rotate back to the left and bring the dumbbell diagonally down toward your left knee.

PLANK SLED PULL
25 YARDS

- Attach a sled to your body with a harness.
- Get in the plank position with Valslides under your feet.
- Walk your hands forward, pulling the sled.

METABOLIC

BATTLE ROPES
THREE SETS OF 40 SECONDS

CHOOSE ONE OF THREE POSSIBILITIES

- Two-handed chops: Make chopping motions while holding the battle ropes, alternating your hands to make waves.

- Slams: Pick up and slam down the battle ropes with both hands.

- Wave lunges: Do two-handed chops while doing forward lunges.

WEEK 10

Welcome to the sport-specific phase. This week, in the movement portion of the workout you will work on your position specifically.

If you are in a specialty position, now is the time to concentrate on routes, catching, blocking, tackling, backpedaling, etc.

If you play offensive or defensive line, it is time to concentrate on blocking, pass rushing, hand placement, tackling and finishing.

For the strength portion, we are going to continue our circuits, slightly decrease the weight and keep our attention on speed. Let's continue to use Wednesday as a recovery day and be sure to rest as much as possible.

Keep up the work! Train hard!

MONDAY

DAILY WARM-UP

- Refer to page 14.

MOVEMENT SERIES

POSITION SPECIFIC

- This series of the program is an opportunity for you as an athlete to choose your own exercises to work on your specific position(s). For example, if you are a wide receiver, work on your route tree; if you are a defensive back, work on press coverage; if you are a defensive end, work on leverage and getting off the ball. This workout can be as long as you feel it needs to be. Our suggestion is no more than an hour long, and be sure to warm up properly before any workout.

CORE SERIES

PILLAR SERIES
30 SECONDS EACH POSITION

- Lie facedown on a bench with your waist at the end so your upper body is hanging over the edge, have a partner sit on your legs at your calves and hold yourself up even with the bench with your arms held to your side.
- With your partner still sitting on your legs at your calves, turn to the right, arms straight at your sides and hold yourself up even with the bench.
- With your partner still sitting on your legs at your calves, turn to the left, arms straight at your sides and hold yourself up even with the bench.
- Turn onto your back, have a partner sit on your legs at your shins, cross your arms across your chest and hold yourself up even with the bench.
- In all four parts of the series, make sure your body is straight and parallel to the ground, even with the bench.

BLOCK 1 (FOUR CIRCUITS)

ROMANIAN DEAD LIFT TO POWER SHRUG
8 REPS

- Hold a bar with your arms extended straight down.
- Bend at the waist and knees until the bar is at mid-shins.
- Bring the bar up quickly, shrugging and lifting your heels off the ground.

BAND SQUAT
10 REPS (FIRST CIRCUIT), 8 REPS (SECOND), 6 REPS (THIRD), 4 REPS (FOURTH)

- Wrap two bands around stationary equipment at about foot height, then attach the other ends to either side of a barbell.
- Get under the barbell in traditional squat position and face away from band.
- Bend at your knees and waist into a near sitting position and then straighten.

SUMO SQUAT TO HAMSTRING STRETCH
6 REPS

- Bend at your knees and waist until you can grab your toes with both hands.
- Bend your knees farther and lower your butt toward the ground.
- Straighten your legs while still holding your toes.

STABILITY BALL ABS
15 REPS

- Put a stability ball under your mid-back to butt.
- Bend your knees and keep your feet flat on the floor. For a greater challenge, hold a dead ball at your chest.
- Do a sit-up.

BLOCK 2 (THREE CIRCUITS)

PLATE ROW
12 REPS

- Stand with your feet shoulder-width apart and a plate in each hand.
- Bend your knees and waist so your torso and thighs are slightly less than 90 degrees.
- Bend your elbows, quickly pulling the plates up toward your armpits.

BAND RDL
8 REPS

- Stand on a band and hold both ends.
- Place your feet shoulder-width apart, and bend your knees and waist.
- Stand and straighten.

LATERAL STRETCH
6 REPS

- Stand with your legs shoulder-width apart.
- Put your right arm on your hip, left arm over your head and bend your body to the right.
- Switch arms and bend your body to the left.

PLATE SIT-UP TO ROTATION
8 REPS EACH SIDE

- Lie down in the sit-up start position holding a plate at your stomach.
- Do a sit-up and rotate fully to the right while holding the plate.
- Rotate back and lie back down to the start position.
- Do another sit-up, rotate to the left and then lie back down.

BLOCK 3 (THREE CIRCUITS)

BAND THRUSTERS
30 SECONDS

- Wrap a band around two stationary pieces of equipment, or use heavy dumbbells as shown in the photos. With your back flat on a bench and perpendicular to the length of the bench, place the band around your hips. Place your feet shoulder-width apart and flat on the ground.
- Lower your hips, thrust upwards to make your hips parallel with your torso, then lower again. Do as many as you can in the allotted time.

REACTIVE MEDICINE BALL WALL THROW
5 REPS EACH SIDE

- Stand a few feet from a wall, bent slightly forward with your right shoulder facing the wall.
- Hold a medicine ball at your waist.
- Jump away from the wall, landing on your left foot with your right leg bent and in the air behind you.
- Jump back toward the wall, landing on your right foot, throw the ball sideways off the wall and catch the rebound.

BARBELL BACK EXTENSION
10 REPS

- Stand with your feet shoulder-width apart.
- Rest a barbell across the back of your shoulders.
- Hold the bar with your hands at shoulder width and your palms facing outward.
- Bend forward at the waist, bending slightly at your knees until your torso is almost parallel to the floor and then straighten.

BATTLE ROPES
30 SECONDS

CHOOSE ONE OF THREE POSSIBILITIES

- Two-handed chops: Make chopping motions while holding the battle ropes, alternating your hands to make waves.

- Slams: Pick up and slam down the battle ropes with both hands.

- Wave lunges: Do two-handed chops while doing forward lunges.

METABOLIC

BAND SQUAT TO WRAP
3 SETS OF 40 SECONDS

- Wrap a band around stationary equipment at about knee height.
- Hold each end and face away from the band.
- Bend at your knees and waist into a near sitting position.
- Straighten your body and arms and bring them up and together, clapping in front of your face.
- Repeat for the allotted time.

TUESDAY

DAILY WARM-UP

- Refer to page 14.

MOVEMENT SERIES

POSITION SPECIFIC

- This series of the program is an opportunity for you as an athlete to choose your own exercises to work on your specific position(s). For example, if you are a wide receiver, work on your route tree; if you are a defensive back, work on press coverage; if you are a defensive end, work on leverage and getting off the ball. This workout can be as long as you feel it needs to be. Our suggestion is no more than an hour long, and be sure to warm up properly before any workout.

CORE SERIES

PUSH-UP SCAPULAR PILLAR SERIES
30 SECONDS, 20 SECONDS EACH POSITION

- Hold your body at the top push-up position for 30 seconds. Lower yourself to the floor, then make a Y with your arms straight, lifting your head, chest, arms and feet off the ground (hold hand weights for a greater challenge). Hold for 20 seconds.
- Lower your body, then move to the midpoint of a push-up and hold for 30 seconds. Lower yourself, then make a T with your arms straight, lifting your head, chest, arms and feet off the ground (hold hand weights for a greater challenge). Hold for 20 seconds.
- Lower your body, then move to the lowest point of a push-up and hold for 30 seconds. Lower yourself, then make a W with your arms, bending your elbows so your hands are at ear level and lifting your head, chest, arms and feet off the ground (hold hand weights for a greater challenge). Hold for 20 seconds. Lower your body.

BLOCK 1 (FOUR CIRCUITS)

KETTLEBELL CLEAN TO ARMPIT
8 REPS

- Stand with your feet shoulder-width apart.
- Bend your knees and waist and hold a kettlebell in each hand at your knees.
- Bend your elbows, pulling the kettlebells up toward your armpits and lifting yourself onto your toes.
- Finish by standing straight and then get back into starting position.

KETTLEBELL SQUAT TO PRESS
12 REPS (FIRST CIRCUIT), 10 REPS (SECOND), 8 REPS (THIRD), 6 REPS (FOURTH)

- Hold two kettlebells at your chest with bent elbows and legs shoulder-width apart.
- Squat, bending at your knees and forward at your waist, and then come up and press the kettlebells over your head with straight arms.

DUMBBELL PUSH-UP TO ROW
8 REPS

- Get in push-up position with your hands on the dumbbells.
- Do a full push-up, down and up.
- Bend your right arm up until the dumbbell is even with your ribs.
- Straighten your arm back down to the ground.
- Bend your left arm up until the dumbbell is even with your ribs.
- Straighten your arm back to the ground.

HEAVY WEIGHTED ABS
15 REPS (START AT 35 POUNDS AND GO UP AS NEEDED)

- Get in sit-up position with your arms bent holding a dumbbell or powerblock on your chest even with your shoulders.
- Do a sit-up, touching your elbows to your thighs and then going back down.

BLOCK 2 (THREE CIRCUITS)

REVERSE LUNGE WITH PLATE RAISE
5 REPS EACH LEG

- Stand straight with your feet apart not quite at shoulder-width.
- Hold a plate in your hands in front of you with your arms straight.
- Step back with your left leg into a lunge, balancing on your left toes and bending your right knee.
- Lift the plate over your head.
- Bring the plate back down and straighten.

PLATE SHRUGS
25 REPS

- Stand straight with your feet slightly apart.
- Hold a plate in each hand with your arms straight at your sides.
- Shrug your shoulders.

ARNOLD PRESS
8 REPS

- Sit on a bench that has a back.
- Place your legs apart, feet flat on the ground, and hold a dumbbell in each hand with your elbows bent and your arms almost at shoulder height.
- Bring the dumbbells together in front of your face until they touch.
- Separate your arms again to the starting position.
- Straighten your arms toward the ceiling, pressing the dumbbells into the air.
- Bend your elbows, bringing your arms back down to the starting position.

THREE-WAY MEDICINE BALL PUSH-UP
5 REPS

- With your body in push-up position, balance each hand on a medicine ball and both feet on a third one.
- Do push-ups.

BLOCK 3 (THREE CIRCUITS)

BATTLE ROPE ALTERNATING WAVES
20 REPS EACH SIDE

- Hold the end of a battle rope in each hand and alternately bring them up and down to create waves.

BATTLE ROPE SLAMS
20 REPS

- Hold one rope in each hand, bring them up and slam them down.

BATTLE ROPE SKIERS
20 REPS EACH SIDE

- Hold the end of a battle rope in each hand.
- Swing one arm up while kicking the opposite leg back.
- Alternate and swing the other arm up and opposite leg back.

TRICEPS KICKBACK
30 SECONDS

- Attach a band to a bar on a bench or other stationary object.
- Stand a few feet away facing the bench holding the ends of the band.
- Bend your knees slightly, bend at the waist and straighten your arms until they are extended fully behind your body and return them to the starting position.
- Repeat as often as possible in the allotted time.

METABOLIC

PULL-UP HOLD
3 REPS AT 40 SECONDS

- Hold a pull-up bar with a neutral grip, palms facing each other.
- Do a pull-up and hold it for 40 seconds.

WEDNESDAY

DAILY WARM-UP

- Refer to page 14.

RECOVERY

- Use a foam roller to go over all your soft tissue.

TONY HILLS

Offensive Tackle
#76 New Orleans Saints
6-5, 305 pounds
Past teams: Pittsburgh Steelers, Denver Broncos, Indianapolis Colts, Dallas Cowboys

I chose Nine Innovations because, at the midpoint of my career, I wanted a different way to train. I was tired of banging away at the weights. I wanted to increase stability and explosion. The first day I worked out with Abdul and was on the ground struggling to get up, I knew that this was the place for me. The benefits of the program are simple—explosiveness, stability and joint integrity. The program has prolonged my career because I'm still able to maintain my explosion without putting my body through the stress of weight bearing every day.

Abdul's program teaches you a different way to work out and, in my opinion, a smarter way. I would recommend it to anybody who is looking for a change to training other than the norm.

THURSDAY

DAILY WARM-UP

- Refer to page 14.

MOVEMENT SERIES

POSITION SPECIFIC

- This series of the program is an opportunity for you as an athlete to choose your own exercises to work on your specific position(s). For example, if you are a wide receiver, work on your route tree; if you are a defensive back, work on press coverage; if you are a defensive end, work on leverage and getting off the ball. This workout can be as long as you feel it needs to be. Our suggestion is no more than an hour long, and be sure to warm up properly before any workout.

CORE SERIES

SEATED MEDICINE BALL THROWS
THREE SETS OF 20 REPS

- From a seated position on the floor, throw a medicine ball back and forth with a partner two to three yards away.
- If there is no partner available, throw the ball against the wall.

BLOCK 1 (FOUR CIRCUITS)

BARBELL HIGH PULL/CLEAN/PRESS
3 REPS EACH SIDE

- Stand straight, legs shoulder-width apart
- Hold a barbell with your palms facing your body.
- Bend your elbows, bring the barbell up to your chest and then straight back down.
- Bend your elbows and flip up so your palms are facing up and the barbell is up to your shoulders, then straighten your arms and lift the barbell over your head.

BARBELL INCLINE
10 REPS (FIRST CIRCUIT), 8 REPS (SECOND), 6 REPS (THIRD), 4 REPS (FOURTH)

- With a bench inclined, lift a barbell off the rack, bring it down to your chest and then back up.

STABILITY BALL BAND PUSH-UP
10 REPS

- Wrap a band around your back with each hand holding on to an end of the band.
- Place your feet up on a stability ball behind you.
- Do a push-up.

TRIGGER POINT
6 REPS

- Place a trigger point block and a ball against the wall.
- Push the ball against the block with your pectoral muscle.
- Have your arm almost at shoulder height with your elbow bent at 90 degrees and your hand toward the ceiling.
- Raise your arm up, moving your shoulder up without straightening your elbow, and then down so the ball rolls along your pec muscle.

BLOCK 2 (THREE CIRCUITS)

BARBELL OVERHEAD RESISTANCE LUNGE
8 REPS EACH LEG

- Hold a barbell over your head.
- Have a band wrapped around your waist and held by a partner pulling back and applying resistance or wrapped around a stationary object.
- Stand straight with your feet about shoulder-width apart.
- Step forward with your right leg, bend your right knee and dip your left knee down.

QUAD HIP FLEXOR STRETCH
6 REPS EACH SIDE

- Place your right knee bent on an Airex pad that is on the ground and rest the top of your right foot on a stability ball or bench so that the bottom of the foot is facing the ceiling. Your left leg should be in front in a bent position.
- Lean forward, bending your left knee forward and reaching your right arm diagonally into the air.

EGG CRADLES
15 REPS

- Lie on your back on the ground, bring your knees and feet together and your hands behind your head.
- Have your partner hold your feet down on the floor.
- Rock your body up, keeping your body curled.
- Have your partner continue to hold your feet but let them rock up.

BLOCK 3 (THREE CIRCUITS)

DEAD BALL BROAD JUMP
5 REPS

- Stand straight and hold a dead ball at your waist. With straight arms, swing the ball over your head.
- Bring it down to your stomach, bending your elbows, knees and waist to prepare to jump.
- Jump and push your arms straight in front of you, throwing the ball as you jump.

WIDE-LEGGED SEATED KETTLEBELL ROTATIONAL PRESS
8 REPS

- Sit with your legs spread into a wide V in front of you.
- Hold a kettlebell in each hand at shoulder height with bent elbows.
- Straighten your right arm up and out, in front of your head on a diagonal.
- Bring it down and repeat with the opposite arm.

BARBELL SQUAT TO PRESS
10 REPS

- Stand straight and hold a barbell resting on your chest underneath your chin.
- Keeping the bar in that position, squat down.
- Once you have come back up from the squat, press the bar over your head. Lower the barbell to your chest and repeat.

JUMP ROPE
2 MINUTES

- Jump rope for 2 minutes.

METABOLIC

INCLINE BAND FLIES
THREE SETS OF 30 SECONDS

- Wrap a band underneath the base of an incline bench, lie back on it and hold an end in each hand with your arms extended to the sides at chest height.
- Keeping your arms straight, bring your hands together then back out to the side.
- Do as many as possible in 30 seconds.

FRIDAY

DAILY WARM-UP

- Refer to page 14.

MOVEMENT SERIES

POSITION SPECIFIC

- This series of the program is an opportunity for you as an athlete to choose your own exercises to work on your specific position(s). For example, if you are a wide receiver, work on your route tree; if you are a defensive back, work on press coverage; if you are a defensive end, work on leverage and getting off the ball. This workout can be as long as you feel it needs to be. Our suggestion is no more than an hour long, and be sure to warm up properly before any workout.

CORE SERIES

PAD PUNCHES
20 REPS EACH POSITION

POSITION 1

- Get into a sit-up position and have your partner hold an Airex pad even with your left hip and at a height so the middle of the pad is about shoulder height at the top of a sit-up. Do a sit-up, turn left and hit the pad with an open right hand.

POSITION 2

- Have your partner move to your right side.
- Do a sit-up, turn right and hit the pad with an open left hand.

POSITION 3

- Have your partner stand at your feet.
- Do a sit-up and hit the pad with both open hands.

BLOCK 1 (FOUR CIRCUITS)

3-POSITION CLEAN
3 REPS

- Stand straight and hold a barbell with straight arms.
- Bend down a little until the barbell is at the top of your thigh.
- Jump slightly and bend your knees, waist and elbows, bringing the barbell up to your shoulders, gripping it so your palms are facing upward.
- Bring the barbell back down.
- Bend forward a little until the barbell is at the midpoint of your thigh.
- Jump slightly and bend your knees, waist and elbows, bringing the barbell up to your shoulders, gripping it so your palms are facing upward.
- Bring the barbell back down.
- Bend forward until the barbell is just below your knees.
- Jump slightly and bend your knees, waist and elbows, bringing the barbell up to your shoulders, gripping it so your palms are facing upward.
- Bring the barbell back down.

FRONT SQUAT
10 REPS (FIRST CIRCUIT), 8 REPS (SECOND), 6 REPS (THIRD), 4 REPS (FOURTH)

- Rest a bar on top of your chest. Squat down as far as you can.

BIKE
30 SECONDS (FIRST CIRCUIT), 45 SECONDS (SECOND), 60 SECONDS (THIRD), 75 SECONDS (FOURTH)

- Bike as fast as possible for the allotted time.

QUAD HIP FLEXOR STRETCH
6 REPS EACH SIDE

- Place your right knee bent on an Airex pad that is on the ground and rest the top of your right foot on a stability ball or bench so that the bottom of the foot is facing the ceiling. Your left leg should be in front in a bent position.
- Lean forward, bending your left knee forward and reaching your right arm diagonally into the air.

BLOCK 2 (THREE CIRCUITS)

FORWARD AND BACKWARD LUNGE WITH ROTATION
5 REPS EACH SIDE

- Holding a plate at your chest, step forward with your right leg, do a forward lunge and rotate your body to the right.
- Come back to standing.
- Step backward with your left leg, do a back lunge and rotate your body to the left.

NEUTRAL PULL-UP
10 REPS

- With a neutral grip, do pull-ups.

BATTLE ROPE SLAMS
30 REPS

- Hold one rope in each hand, bring them up and slam them down.

PLATE HOLDS
30 SECONDS

- Sit on the floor with your legs straight.
- Take a plate and lean back, lift your legs off the ground, bring the plate up with straight arms and hold it diagonally in front of your face.
- Hold for 30 seconds.

BLOCK 3 (THREE CIRCUITS)

INCLINE FLY 1¹/₂
30 SECONDS

- Sit back on an inclined bench.
- Hold a dumbbell in each hand with your arms out at shoulder height.
- Bring your arms all the way together in front of your chest, back out to the sides and then halfway to the middle and back out to sides.
- Repeat for the allotted time.

BAND ROW 1¹/₂
30 SECONDS

- Wrap a band around stationary equipment at about waist height.
- Hold the ends in both hands, palms facing down.
- Bend at your knees and waist into a near sitting position that puts the band at chest height.
- Pull back, bending your elbows and turning your hands 90 degrees so your palms are facing each other.
- Pull all the way back until your hands are at your body and then straighten your arms again.
- Pull back halfway to your body and then straighten your arms.
- Repeat for the allotted time.

TRI EXTENSION 1¹/₂
30 SECONDS

- Stand with your feet shoulder-width apart.
- Hold one dumbbell with both hands, your arms up and your elbows near your ears bent so the dumbbell is behind your back.
- Straighten your arms, bringing the dumbbell over your head.
- Bend your arms, bringing the dumbbell halfway down.
- Straighten your arms back up and then bend them all the way to return to the start position.
- Do as any as possible in the allotted time.

BICEPS CURL 1¹/₂
30 SECONDS

- Stand straight, holding a bar with your arms down and palms turned out.
- Bend your elbows, curling the bar to your chest.
- Straighten your arms then bring the bar back up halfway and straighten your arms again.
- Do as many times as possible in the allotted time.

METABOLIC

TREADMILL
THREE SETS OF 40 SECONDS

- Run as fast as possible for the allotted time.

WEEK 11

You are a third of the way through the last phase! Congratulations. It's been a great off-season for you. Let's continue to push ourselves. The season favors those who are prepared, and you will be!

We are going to continue our movement with position-specific workouts. The beauty of this game is being able to find your style. Feel free to get creative while working on the techniques and movements of your position.

We'll continue our circuits with the same weight and speed.

Keep it up! Train hard!

MONDAY

DAILY WARM-UP

- Refer to page 14.

MOVEMENT SERIES

POSITION SPECIFIC

- This series of the program is an opportunity for you as an athlete to choose your own exercises to work on your specific position(s). For example, if you are a wide receiver, work on your route tree; if you are a defensive back, work on press coverage; if you are a defensive end, work on leverage and getting off the ball. This workout can be as long as you feel it needs to be. Our suggestion is no more than an hour long, and be sure to warm up properly before any workout.

CORE SERIES

PILLAR SERIES
30 SECONDS EACH POSITION

- Lie facedown on a bench with your waist at the end so your upper body is hanging over the edge, have a partner sit on your legs at your calves and hold yourself up even with the bench with your arms held to your side.
- With your partner still sitting on your legs at your calves, turn to the right, arms straight at your sides and hold yourself up even with the bench.
- With your partner still sitting on your legs at your calves, turn to the left, arms straight at your sides and hold yourself up even with the bench.
- Turn onto your back, have a partner sit on your legs at your shins, cross your arms across your chest and hold yourself up even with the bench.
- In all four parts of the series, make sure your body is straight and parallel to the ground, even with the bench.

BLOCK 1 (FOUR CIRCUITS)

SINGLE-ARM DUMBBELL SNATCH TO PRESS
4 REPS EACH ARM

- Stand with your feet shoulder-width apart and a dumbbell horizontally between them.
- Bend down and grab the dumbbell with your right hand.
- In one motion, jump and lift the dumbbell over your head.
- Bend your elbow, bringing the dumbbell to your shoulder and then press it over your head, straightening your arm.
- Bend at the waist until the dumbbell touches the floor.

INCLINE BENCH
10 REPS (FIRST CIRCUIT), 8 REPS (SECOND), 6 REPS (THIRD), 4 REPS (FOURTH)

- Lie back on an inclined bench with your feet flat on the floor.
- Bring a bar down to your chest and then back up.

STANDING TS
6 REPS EACH LEG

- Get in forward lunge position with your right leg in front and left leg in back.
- Keep your waist and torso straight.
- Hold your arms straight and out to the side (like a T).
- Bring them together in front of your face and open them back up.

MEDICINE BALL CHEST PASS
30 SECONDS

- Hold a medicine ball at your chest, push and throw it to a partner. If you don't have a partner, throw the ball into a wall.

BLOCK 2 (THREE CIRCUITS)

WALKING LUNGE, PUSH-UP TO ROTATION
8 REPS

- Step forward with your right leg and do a forward lunge.
- Move into the push-up position and do a push-up then lift your right arm in the air and rotate your body to the right.
- Stand up and step forward with your left leg and do a forward lunge.
- Move your right leg back and put your hands down into the push-up position, do a push-up and then lift your left arm in the air and rotate your body to the left.
- That is 1 rep.

KETTLEBELL ECCENTRIC ROW
8 REPS

- Stand with your legs shoulder-width apart.
- Bend your knees and waist slightly.
- Hold a kettlebell in each hand and bend your elbows to bring the kettlebells up to your waist in one second.
- Lower the kettlebells slowly, taking five seconds.

DUMBBELL PUSH-UP TO ROW
8 REPS

- Get in push-up position with your hands on the dumbbells.
- Do a full push-up, down and up.
- Bend your right arm up until the dumbbell is even with your ribs.
- Straighten your arm back down to the ground.
- Bend your left arm up until the dumbbell is even with your ribs.
- Straighten your arm back to the ground.

PLATE SIT-UPS
15 REPS

- In the sit-up start position, hold a plate over your chest with straight arms.
- Do a sit-up and at the top of it, push your arms back so the plate is over your head.
- Lie back down while returning your arms to the starting position, holding the plate over your chest with your arms straight.

BLOCK 3 (THREE CIRCUITS)

JUNGLE GYM (OR TRX) STABILITY BALL PUSH-UP
10 REPS

- Place feet in TRX stirrups and rest your chest on a stability ball. The stirrups should be at the same height as the stability ball.
- Put your hands on the ball and do push-ups.

LATERAL HURDLE TO PUSH SLED
1 REP EACH SIDE

- Set up a mini hurdle a few feet behind a sled, lining up the hurdle with the left side of the sled.
- Stand to the left of the mini hurdle.
- Jump over the hurdle and then push the sled for five yards.
- Switch the hurdle to the right side of the sled and stand to the right of it.
- Jump over the hurdle and then push the sled for five yards.

MEDICINE BALL REVERSE THROW
5 REPS

- Stand holding a medicine ball at your waist with your feet shoulder-width apart.
- Bend down swinging the medicine ball slightly between your legs and then come up and throw it backward over your head.

HIPS ELEVATED ALTERNATE MARCH
10 REPS

- Lie on your back on the floor with your arms to your sides, palms down, knees bent and feet on the floor.
- Raise your hips into the air.
- Keeping your hips in the air, lift your left leg into the air, bringing your knee toward your chest and keeping it bent at 90 degrees.
- Lower your leg to the floor, keeping your hips raised and knee bent.
- Repeat with the right leg.
- That is 1 rep.

METABOLIC

BAND HIGH PULL
THREE SETS OF 40 SECONDS

- Wrap a band around the base of a bench.
- Stand straight and hold both ends of the band with your palms facing down.
- Pull toward your face, bending your elbows straight out and finishing with your hands at your face and arms bent and at a 90-degree angle from your body before straightening your arms again.
- Repeat for the allotted time.

TUESDAY

DAILY WARM-UP

- Refer to page 14.

MOVEMENT SERIES

POSITION SPECIFIC

- This series of the program is an opportunity for you as an athlete to choose your own exercises to work on your specific position(s). For example, if you are a wide receiver, work on your route tree; if you are a defensive back, work on press coverage; if you are a defensive end, work on leverage and getting off the ball. This workout can be as long as you feel it needs to be. Our suggestion is no more than an hour long, and be sure to warm up properly before any workout.

CORE SERIES

PUSH-UP SCAPULAR PILLAR SERIES
30 SECONDS. 20 SECONDS EACH POSITION

- Hold your body at the top push-up position for 30 seconds. Lower yourself to the floor, then make a Y with your arms straight, lifting your head, chest, arms and feet off the ground (hold hand weights for a greater challenge). Hold for 20 seconds.

- Lower your body, then move to the midpoint of a push-up and hold for 30 seconds. Lower yourself, then make a T with your arms straight, lifting your head, chest, arms and feet off the ground (hold hand weights for a greater challenge). Hold for 20 seconds.

- Lower your body, then move to the lowest point of a push-up and hold for 30 seconds. Lower yourself, then make a W with your arms, bending your elbows so your hands are at ear level and lifting your head, chest, arms and feet off the ground (hold hand weights for a greater challenge). Hold for 20 seconds. Lower your body.

BLOCK 1 (FOUR CIRCUITS)

BARBELL HIGH PULL, SNATCH, ROW, FORWARD LUNGE
5 REPS

- Stand with your legs shoulder-width apart, holding a barbell with your palms facing your body.
- Bend your knees slightly and then bend your elbows to lift the bar to your chest in a high pull. Do this twice.
- With the same motion as the high pull, lift the bar over your head twice.
- Bend your knees about 45 degrees and bend your waist, pushing your butt back, lean forward and row the bar twice, bending your elbows and pulling the bar into your body.
- Stand straight and place the bar behind your neck on your shoulders with your palms out and do a forward lunge, first stepping forward with your right leg, then back to the start position and then step forward with left leg.

BARBELL STEP-UP
10 REPS (FIRST CIRCUIT), 8 REPS (SECOND), 6 REPS (THIRD), 4 REPS (FOURTH)

- Hold a barbell on your shoulders behind your neck.
- Step up on a plyo box with your right leg, bend and bring up your left knee, and then step down with your left leg.
- Repeat stepping up with your left leg and bringing your right knee into the air.

QUAD HIP FLEXOR STRETCH
6 REPS EACH SIDE

- Place your right knee bent on an Airex pad that is on the ground and rest the top of your right foot on a stability ball or bench so that the bottom of the foot is facing the ceiling. Your left leg should be in front in a bent postion.
- Lean forward, bending your left knee forward and reaching your right arm diagonally into the air.

PLATE SIT-UPS
15 REPS

- In the sit-up start position, hold a plate over your chest with straight arms.
- Do a sit-up and at the top of it, push your arms back so the plate is over your head.
- Lie back down while returning your arms to the starting position, holding the plate over your chest with your arms straight.

BLOCK 2 (FOUR CIRCUITS)

DUMBBELL BENCH HIPS OFF
5 REPS

- With only your head and shoulders on the bench, knees bent, feet flat on floor and a dumbbell in each hand, hold your arms straight up.
- Bend your elbow, bring the dumbbell to your shoulder and then straighten your arm, pressing the dumbbell back up.
- You can alternate arms or do them together.

GLUTE ACTIVATION
15 REPS EACH SIDE, THEN 15 WITH BOTH LEGS TOGETHER

- Wrap mini bands around your knees and ankles, and get down in a squat position without letting your knees go past your toes.
- Turn your right knee out, pushing against the band's resistance. Turn your right knee back in, then turn out your left knee. Finally, turn both knees out together.

BOX JUMP TWO TO ONE
3 REPS EACH SIDE

- Stand a couple of feet from a plyo box, facing it.
- Swing your arms from over your head to down past your sides while bending your knees and waist.
- Jump off with both feet and land on the box on your right foot.
- Do 3 reps and then repeat landing on your left foot.

90-DEGREE PULL-UP HOLD
30 SECONDS

- Hold a pull-up bar with a neutral grip and your palms facing each other.
- Pull yourself up until your elbows are bent at 90 degrees.
- Hold for 30 seconds.

BLOCK 3 (FOUR CIRCUITS)

FRONT FOOT ELEVATED LUNGE WITH ROTATION
8 REPS EACH LEG

- Put your right foot flat on a plyo box and hold a medicine ball at your waist.
- Lean forward and lunge and when your right knee is farthest forward, twist to the right, return to center and then push back to the start position.

SINGLE-LEGGED MEDICINE BALL SLAMS
5 REPS EACH LEG

- Stand straight, legs close together, holding a medicine ball at stomach level.
- Lift your left foot slightly off the ground.
- Raise the ball over your head and bring it down, bending at the waist and slamming it to the ground.

FARMER'S WALK
50 YARDS

- With kettlebells in each hand and arms at your sides, walk forward.

KETTLEBELL SIT-UP TO ROTATIONAL PRESS
8 REPS

- Get in the sit-up start position with a kettlebell in each hand and your elbows bent so the kettlebells are at your shoulders.
- Do a sit-up and at the height of the sit-up extend your right arm diagonally up and across in front of your face and then bring it down.
- Extend your left arm and do the same.
- Lower yourself back to the start position.

METABOLIC

BAND SQUAT TO WRAP
THREE SETS OF 40 SECONDS

- Wrap a band around stationary equipment at about knee height.
- Hold each end and face away from the band.
- Bend at your knees and waist into a near sitting position.
- Straighten your body and arms and bring them up and together, clapping in front of your face.
- Repeat for the allotted time.

WEDNESDAY

DAILY WARM-UP

- Refer to page 14.

RECOVERY

- Use a foam roller to go over all your soft tissue.

THURSDAY

DAILY WARM-UP

- Refer to page 14.

MOVEMENT SERIES

POSITION SPECIFIC

- This series of the program is an opportunity for you as an athlete to choose your own exercises to work on your specific position(s). For example, if you are a wide receiver, work on your route tree; if you are a defensive back, work on press coverage; if you are a defensive end, work on leverage and getting off the ball. This workout can be as long as you feel it needs to be. Our suggestion is no more than an hour long, and be sure to warm up properly before any workout.

CORE SERIES

SEATED MEDICINE BALL THROWS
THREE SETS OF 20 REPS

- From a seated position on the floor, throw a medicine ball back and forth with a partner two to three yards away.
- If there is no partner available, throw the ball against the wall.

BLOCK 1 (FOUR CIRCUITS)

BARBELL HIGH PULL/CLEAN
4 REPS

- Stand straight with your legs shoulder-width apart.
- Hold a bar with your palms facing your body.
- Bend your elbows and bring the bar up to your chest and then straight back down.
- Bend your elbows and flip up so your palms are facing up and the bar is up to your shoulders and then straighten back down.

WEIGHTED PULL-UPS
8 REPS (FIRST CIRCUIT), 6 REPS (SECOND), 6 REPS (THIRD), 4 REPS (FOURTH)

- Hold a pull-up bar with a neutral grip.
- Bend your knees to 90 degrees, keep your legs together and hold a dead ball between your legs or rest it on your thighs.
- Do pull-ups.

PLATE FRONT RAISERS
10 REPS

- Stand with your legs shoulder-width apart.
- Hold a plate with both hands in front of your body with straight arms.
- Lift the plate with your arms straight until the plate is in front of your face, then lift it above your head.
- Lower your arms back to the starting position.

PEANUT
6 REPS

- Lie on the floor so the peanut is between your scapular muscles.
- Have your body straight, feet apart, arms straight up in the air and palms together.
- Lower your straight right arm past your head until your hand touches the ground and then bring it back up.
- Lower your straight left arm past your head until your hand touches the ground and then bring it back up.
- Open your arms, lowering them each to a side even with your shoulders until your hands touch the ground and then bring them back up to the starting position.

BLOCK 2 (THREE CIRCUITS)

DEAD BALL TRANSVERSE LATERAL STEP-UP
8 REPS EACH SIDE

- Place a plyo box two feet behind you and to the left.
- Stand straight with your back to the box.
- Holding a dead ball with both hands at your chest, turn and step onto the box with your left leg.
- Bend your knee and bring your right leg up.
- Step back down.

QUAD HIP FLEXOR STRETCH
6 REPS EACH SIDE

- Place your right knee bent on an Airex pad that is on the ground and rest the top of your right foot on a stability ball or bench so that the bottom of the foot is facing the ceiling. Your left leg should be in front in a bent position.
- Lean forward, bending your left knee forward and reaching your right arm diagonally into the air.

SLED PULL
25 YARDS

- Pull a sled for 25 yards.

STABILITY BALL ABS
30 SECONDS

- Put a stability ball under your mid-back to butt.
- Bend your knees and keep your feet flat on the floor. For a greater challenge, hold a dead ball at your chest.
- Do as many sit-ups as possible for the allotted time.

BLOCK 3 (THREE CIRCUITS)

DUMBBELL PUSH-UP TO ROW
8 REPS

- Get in push-up position with your hands on the dumbbells.
- Do a full push-up, down and up.
- Bend your right arm up until the dumbbell is even with your ribs.
- Straighten your arm back down to the ground.
- Bend your left arm up until the dumbbell is even with your ribs.
- Straighten your arm back to the ground.

SPLIT-STANCE MEDICINE BALL OVERHEAD SLAMS
5 REPS EACH SIDE

- With your right leg forward, knee bent at 90 degrees, and your left leg back balanced on your toes in the lunge position, hold a medicine ball at your waist, then bring it around to the left, swing it over your head while holding the ball with both hands and come down and slam the ball off the ground.
- Catch the ball on the bounce and swing it over your head to the right, bouncing it off the ground and catching it again.

SINGLE-LEGGED ABDOMINAL SLIDERS
15 REPS EACH LEG

- Put a Valslide under each foot.
- Get in the plank position with your arms straight and hands on the floor.
- Bend your right knee and slide your leg all the way forward and then back.

METABOLIC

TIRE FLIPS
THREE SETS OF 40 SECONDS

- Flip a tire as many times as possible in the allotted time.

FRIDAY

DAILY WARM-UP

- Refer to page 14.

MOVEMENT SERIES

POSITION SPECIFIC

- This series of the program is an opportunity for you as an athlete to choose your own exercises to work on your specific position(s). For example, if you are a wide receiver, work on your route tree; if you are a defensive back, work on press coverage; if you are a defensive end, work on leverage and getting off the ball. This workout can be as long as you feel it needs to be. Our suggestion is no more than an hour long, and be sure to warm up properly before any workout.

PAD PUNCHES
20 REPS EACH POSITION

POSITION 1

- Get into a sit-up position and have your partner hold an Airex pad even with your left hip and at a height so the middle of the pad is about shoulder height at the top of a sit-up. Do a sit-up, turn left and hit the pad with an open right hand.

POSITION 2

- Have your partner move to your right side.
- Do a sit-up, turn right and hit the pad with an open left hand.

POSITION 3

- Have your partner stand at your feet.
- Do a sit-up and hit the pad with both open hands.

BLOCK 1 (FOUR CIRCUITS)

BAND SQUAT
30 SECONDS

- Wrap two bands around stationary equipment at about foot height, then attach the other ends to either side of a barbell.
- Get under the barbell in traditional squat position and face away from band.
- Bend at your knees and waist into a near sitting position and then straighten.
- Do as many as possible in the allotted time.

BIKE
30 SECONDS

- Bike as fast as possible for the allotted time.

SPEED BARBELL BAND BENCH
30 SECONDS

- Attach a band from the bottom of a bench to each side of the bar.
- Bench press, bringing the bar all the way down to your chest and back up as fast as possible for the allotted time.

KETTLEBELL BALLISTIC ROW
30 SECONDS

- Bend your knees and waist.
- Hold a kettlebell in your right hand and put your left hand on your hip.
- Bend your elbow, bringing the kettlebell up and letting go when it's at your waist.
- Catch it with your left hand while moving your right hand to your hip.
- Lower the kettelbell, bring it back up then let go and grab it with your right hand.
- Do as many reps as possible in the allotted time.

BLOCK 2 (THREE CIRCUITS)

BATTLE ROPES
30 SECONDS

CHOOSE ONE OF THREE POSSIBILITIES

- Two-handed chops: Make chopping motions while holding the battle ropes, alternating your hands to make waves.

- Slams: Pick up and slam down the battle ropes with both hands.

- Wave lunges: Do two-handed chops while doing forward lunges.

TRICEPS KICKBACK
30 SECONDS

- Attach a band to a bar on a bench or other stationary object.
- Stand a few feet away facing the bench and holding the ends of the band.
- Bend your knees slightly, bend at the waist and straighten your arms until they are extended fully behind your body and return them to the starting position.
- Repeat as often as possible in the allotted time.

BAND BI (BICEP CURLS WITH BAND)
30 SECONDS

- Wrap a TRX band around the base of a bench or another stationary object.
- Stand straight and hold each handle of the band with your palms down.
- Bend your elbows up into a biceps curl while turning your hands until your palms are up.
- Straighten your arms back down.
- Repeat for the allotted time.

BLOCK 3 (THREE CIRCUITS)

PLANK BALL ROLL
30 SECONDS EACH DIRECTION

- Put your elbows and forearms on a stability ball with your palms facing up.
- Get in the plank position and up on your toes.
- Move your arms in circles to the right, rolling the ball.

90-DEGREE PULL-UP HOLD
30 SECONDS

- Hold a pull-up bar with a neutral grip and your palms facing each other.
- Pull yourself up until your elbows are bent at 90 degrees.
- Hold for 30 seconds.

METABOLIC

BENCH
THREE SETS OF 40 SECONDS

- Do as many bench presses as possible in the allotted time.

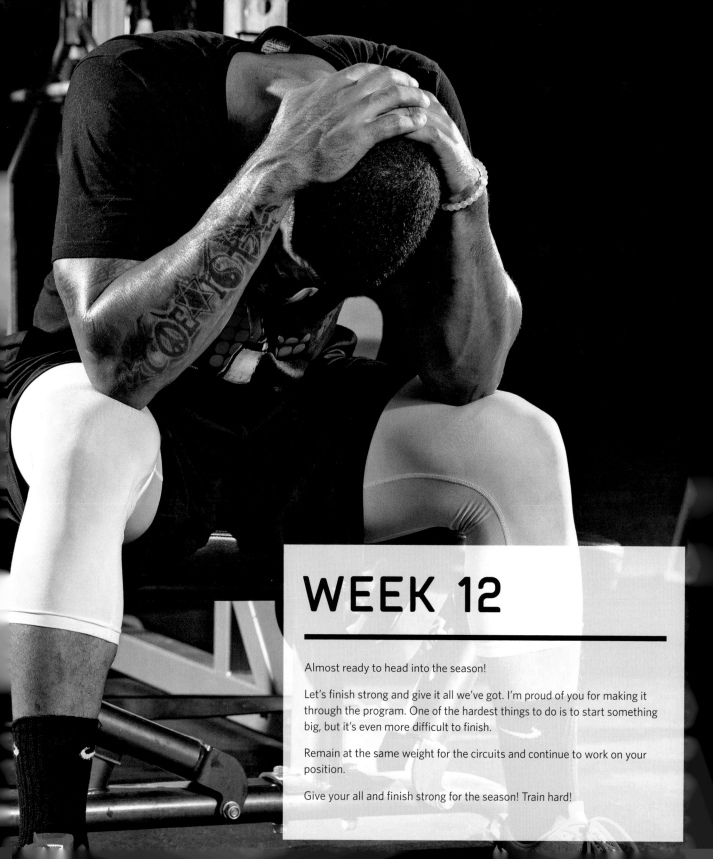

WEEK 12

Almost ready to head into the season!

Let's finish strong and give it all we've got. I'm proud of you for making it through the program. One of the hardest things to do is to start something big, but it's even more difficult to finish.

Remain at the same weight for the circuits and continue to work on your position.

Give your all and finish strong for the season! Train hard!

MONDAY

DAILY WARM-UP

- Refer to page 14.

MOVEMENT SERIES

POSITION SPECIFIC

- This series of the program is an opportunity for you as an athlete to choose your own exercises to work on your specific position(s). For example, if you are a wide receiver, work on your route tree; if you are a defensive back, work on press coverage; if you are a defensive end, work on leverage and getting off the ball. This workout can be as long as you feel it needs to be. Our suggestion is no more than an hour long, and be sure to warm up properly before any workout.

CORE SERIES

PILLAR SERIES
30 SECONDS EACH POSITION

- Lie facedown on a bench with your waist at the end so your upper body is hanging over the edge, have a partner sit on your legs at your calves and hold yourself up even with the bench with your arms held to your side.
- With your partner still sitting on your legs at your calves, turn to the right, arms straight at your sides and hold yourself up even with the bench.
- With your partner still sitting on your legs at your calves, turn to the left, arms straight at your sides and hold yourself up even with the bench.
- Turn onto your back, have a partner sit on your legs at your shins, cross your arms across your chest and hold yourself up even with the bench.
- In all four parts of the series, make sure your body is straight and parallel to the ground, even with the bench.

BLOCK 1 (FOUR CIRCUITS)

SNATCH GRIP HIGH PULL
8 REPS

- Stand straight with your legs slightly more than shoulder-width apart.
- Hold a barbell with your palms down and your hands about six inches wider than your hips.
- Bend forward at the waist and slightly at the knees, bend your elbows and quickly pull the barbell up to your chest and back down.

BARBELL BENCH
10 REPS (FIRST CIRCUIT), 8 REPS (SECOND), 6 REPS (THIRD), 4 REPS (FOURTH)

- Bench press for the specified number of reps.

PLATE FRONT RAISERS
10 REPS

- Stand with your legs shoulder-width apart.
- Hold a plate with both hands in front of your body with straight arms.
- Lift the plate with your arms straight until the plate is in front of your face, then lift it above your head.
- Lower your arms back to the starting position.

AB ROLLOUT
15 REPS

- Start with your knees on an Airex pad, legs slightly separated and shins flat to ground. Hold an ab roller directly in front of you and roll to full extension, and then roll it back.

BLOCK 2 (THREE CIRCUITS)

IPSILATERAL KETTLEBELL STEP-UP TO PRESS
5 REPS EACH SIDE

- Hold a kettlebell in your left hand.
- Step up onto a plyo box with your left foot and raise your right knee until it's bent 90 degrees.
- Press the kettlebell toward the ceiling.
- Bring the kettlebell back down and step down off the box.

BAND RDL
8 REPS

- Stand on a band and hold both ends.
- Place your feet shoulder-width apart, and bend your knees and waist.
- Stand and straighten.

BENT KNEE HAMSTRING STRETCH
6 REPS EACH LEG

- Lie flat on your back on the floor with your legs straight.
- Bend your right knee, bringing your leg up and clasping your hands around your hamstring.
- Straighten your leg toward the ceiling and bend it back down.

DEAD BALL WALL THROW
5 REPS

- Get in the sit-up position with your legs separated and your feet a couple of feet from the wall.
- Hold a dead ball with both hands above the space between your thighs.
- Lean back, raise your arms over your head until the ball touches the ground.
- Come up and throw the ball against the wall.
- Pick up the ball and repeat.

BLOCK 3 (THREE CIRCUITS)

KETTLEBELL NEUTRAL LUNGE
5 REPS

- Holding a kettlebell with both hands and your arms down, lunge to the left and back up, then lunge to the right and back up.

DUMBBELL HAMMER CURL
10 REPS

- Stand straight with your legs slightly apart, a dumbbell in each hand and palms facing each other.
- Bend your elbows, keeping your palms facing in and bringing the dumbbells to your shoulders and then lower.

FRONT FOOT ELEVATED SPLIT-STANCE MEDICINE BALL TOSS
10 REPS EACH SIDE

- Place your left leg on an Airex pad, bend your knee and stretch your right leg back in lunge position.
- Hold a medicine ball at your waist, rotate your upper body away from the wall, come back and then throw the ball against the wall and catch it.

90-DEGREE PULL-UP HOLD
30 SECONDS

- Hold a pull-up bar with a neutral grip and your palms facing each other.
- Pull yourself up until your elbows are bent at 90 degrees.
- Hold for 30 seconds.

METABOLIC

BATTLE ROPES
THREE SETS OF 40 SECONDS

CHOOSE ONE OF THREE POSSIBILITIES

- Two-handed chops: Make chopping motions while holding the battle ropes, alternating your hands to make waves.

- Slams: Pick up and slam down the battle ropes with both hands.

(continued)

- Wave lunges: Do two-handed chops while doing forward lunges.

TUESDAY

DAILY WARM-UP

- Refer to page 14.

MOVEMENT SERIES

POSITION SPECIFIC

- This series of the program is an opportunity for you as an athlete to choose your own exercises to work on your specific position(s). For example, if you are a wide receiver, work on your route tree; if you are a defensive back, work on press coverage; if you are a defensive end, work on leverage and getting off the ball. This workout can be as long as you feel it needs to be. Our suggestion is no more than an hour long, and be sure to warm up properly before any workout.

CORE SERIES

PUSH-UP SCAPULAR PILLAR SERIES
20 SECONDS, 10 SECONDS EACH POSITION

- Hold your body at the top push-up position for 20 seconds. Lower yourself to the floor, then make a Y with your arms straight, lifting your head, chest, arms and feet off the ground (hold hand weights for a greater challenge). Hold for 10 seconds.
- Lower your body, then move to the midpoint of a push-up and hold for 20 seconds. Lower yourself, then make a T with your arms straight, lifting your head, chest, arms and feet off the ground (hold hand weights for a greater challenge). Hold for 10 seconds.
- Lower your body, then move to the lowest point of a push-up and hold for 20 seconds. Lower yourself, then make a W with your arms, bending your elbows so your hands are at ear level and lifting your head, chest, arms and feet off the ground (hold hand weights for a greater challenge). Hold for 10 seconds.
- Lower your body and repeat.

BLOCK 1 (FOUR CIRCUITS)

RESISTANCE KETTLEBELL SWING
15 REPS

- Wrap a band through a kettlebell and spread the looped side out on the floor.
- Stretch the band and stand on each side to anchor the band to the floor.
- Stand straight and hold the kettlebell in both hands with your arms straight in front of your body and legs shoulder-width apart.
- Bend your knees and swing the kettlebell through your legs then back up to shoulder height, keeping your arms straight.

WALKING LUNGE WITH ROTATION
10 REPS (FIRST CIRCUIT), 8 REPS (SECOND), 6 REPS (THIRD), 4 REPS (FOURTH)

- Hold a medicine ball at your waist.
- Step forward with your right leg, bending your knee to 90 degrees and dipping your left knee down.
- Rotate your torso to the right and back to center.
- Step forward with your left leg, bending your knee to 90 degrees and dipping your right knee down.
- Rotate your torso to the left and back to center.
- That is 1 rep.

PUSH-PULL SLED
25 YARDS

- Push a sled forward, running for 25 yards, then pull it back, running backward for 25 yards.

JUNGLE GYM/TRX BODY SAW
15 REPS

- Place your feet in TRX band handles, so they hang at shoulder height.
- Extend your body fully and put your elbows and forearms on the ground with your palms up.
- Without moving your elbows, straighten your arms to push your body back and then bring your body forward.

BLOCK 2 (THREE CIRCUITS)

HORIZONTAL ROW
12 REPS

- Place a barbell on a rack about four feet off the floor.
- Hold the bar, gripping past shoulder-width.
- Place your heels on a plyo box with your legs straight.
- Straighten your arms so your body and thighs are even, parallel to the floor.
- Pull your chest up to the bar and straighten your arms back down.

KETTLEBELL REVERSE FLY
15 REPS

- Hold a kettlebell in each hand.
- Bend at your knees and waist with your arms hanging down and the kettlebells at about shin level.
- Keeping your arms straight, bring them out to the side to shoulder height, as if mimicking a wing motion, and then back down.

BATTLE ROPES
30 SECONDS

CHOOSE ONE OF THREE POSSIBILITIES

- Two-handed chops: Make chopping motions while holding the battle ropes, alternating your hands to make waves.

- Slams: Pick up and slam down the battle ropes with both hands.

- Wave lunges: Do two-handed chops while doing forward lunges.

BLOCK 3 (THREE CIRCUITS)

HEAVY DUMBBELL BENCH
5 REPS

- Lie on your back on a bench with your knees bent at the end and feet flat on the ground.
- Hold dumbbells with your elbows bent and the dumbbells at your side, palms pointing upward.
- Straighten your arms all the way up and then bring them all the way back down.

MEDICINE BALL PERPENDICULAR WALL THROW
5 REPS EACH SIDE

- Stand perpendicular to the wall, your left shoulder nearest it about two feet away.
- Hold a ball about stomach height.
- Bend at your knees and twist to the right, away from the wall.
- When turning back to the wall, throw the ball at it and catch the rebound.

LATERAL STEP-UP WITH PLATE EXTENSION
8 REPS EACH SIDE

- Stand to the left side of a plyo box.
- Hold a plate in both hands at your chest.
- Step up with your right foot then your left, straighten your arms extending the plate and then bring it back to your chest.
- Step back down.

GLUTE BRIDGE
30 SECONDS

- Lie on your back on the floor, knees bent, feet flat on the floor.
- With your arms straight down at your sides a little away from your body, your palms down and flat on the floor, raise your hips and toes as high as you can.
- Hold for the allotted time.

METABOLIC

LATERAL PULL DOWN
THREE SETS OF 40 SECONDS

- Sit on the bench of a pull-down machine. Hold the bar at the far ends.
- Lean back slightly and pull the bar down to your chest and then straighten your arms to the start position.
- Do as many as possible in the allotted time.

WEDNESDAY

DAILY WARM-UP

- Refer to page 14.

RECOVERY

- Use a foam roller to go over all your soft tissue.

THURSDAY

DAILY WARM-UP

- Refer to page 14.

MOVEMENT SERIES

POSITION SPECIFIC

- This series of the program is an opportunity for you as an athlete to choose your own exercises to work on your specific position(s). For example, if you are a wide receiver, work on your route tree; if you are a defensive back, work on press coverage; if you are a defensive end, work on leverage and getting off the ball. This workout can be as long as you feel it needs to be. Our suggestion is no more than an hour long, and be sure to warm up properly before any workout.

CORE SERIES

SEATED MEDICINE BALL THROWS
THREE SETS OF 20 REPS

- From a seated position on the floor, throw a medicine ball back and forth with a partner two to three yards away.
- If there is no partner available, throw the ball against the wall.

BLOCK 1 (FOUR CIRCUITS)

THREE POSITION HIGH PULL
3 REPS

- Stand straight and hold a barbell at your waist with your palms facing your body.
- Bend your knees slightly, and bring the bar up to your chest while doing a small jump.
- Bend your knees and slide the bar to mid-thigh and then repeat the high pull.
- Bend your knees more, slide the bar to your knees and then repeat the high pull.

INCLINE DUMBBELL BENCH PRESS (135 POUNDS)
10 REPS

- Lie on your back on a bench with your knees bent at the end, feet flat on the ground.
- Hold dumbbells with your elbows bent and the dumbbells at your side, palms pointing upward.
- Straighten your arms all the way up, and then bring them all the way back down.

MEDICINE BALL CHEST PASS
30 SECONDS

- Hold a medicine ball at your chest, push and throw it to a partner. If you don't have a partner, throw the ball into a wall.

STICK STRETCH
6 REPS EACH SIDE

- Stand with your legs wider than shoulder width.
- Have a stick about an arm's length from your body and hold it at shoulder height in your right hand.
- Bend your knees and waist until your torso is nearly parallel to the ground while still holding the stick.
- Pulse (small bounces) at shoulder/trap at the lowest point of the squat and then stand back up.

BLOCK 2 (THREE CIRCUITS)

BARBELL SINGLE-LEGGED HIP THRUST
5 REPS EACH SIDE

- Lie back with only your head and shoulders on a bench so you're perpendicular to the bench.
- Bend your knees and put your feet flat on the floor.
- Hold a barbell with your palms down at your waist.
- Lift your left leg until it's straight and parallel with the ground.
- Keeping your leg straight and in the air, bend your right knee so your butt lowers toward the floor and then straighten up.

SUMO SQUAT TO HAMSTRING STRETCH
6 REPS

- Bend at your knees and waist until you can grab your toes with both hands.
- Bend your knees farther and lower your butt toward ground.
- Straighten your legs while still holding your toes.

BAND JUMP WITH MEDICINE BALL
5 REPS

- Attach one band to each side of the bottom of a barbell rack. Turn your back toward the rack.
- Take the band from the right side, put the loop over your head and down on your left shoulder.
- Take the band from the left side, put the loop over your head and down on your right shoulder.
- Hold the medicine ball at your chest, bend your knees and then push off and jump.

DUMBBELL SIDE BENDS
15 REPS EACH SIDE

- Stand straight with your feet shoulder-width apart.
- Hold a dumbbell in your left hand at your side with your arm straight.
- Bend your right arm and hold your hand behind your head.
- Lean to the left a few inches.
- Lean back through, straight to the right side.

BLOCK 3 (THREE CIRCUITS)

BASE POSITION TWIST WITH EXTENSION
10 REPS EACH SIDE

- Attach a band to stationary equipment just below shoulder height.
- Stand perpendicular to the equipment with your right shoulder closest and your legs shoulder-width apart, knees slightly bent.
- Hold the outstretched band in both hands at chest level with your arms straight.
- Twist your torso to the left, then twist back to center. Bring the band into your chest and then straighten your arms to return to the start position.

TRIPOD PUSH-UPS
30 SECONDS

- Get in a normal push-up position.
- Lift your right foot, resting it on your left foot with your right toes on your left heel, and lower your body to the ground and back up.
- Put your right foot down and lift your left foot, resting it on your right foot with your right toes on your right heel, and lower your body to the ground and back up.
- Repeat as often as possible in the allotted time.

HEAVY WEIGHTED ABS
15 REPS (START AT 35 POUNDS AND GO UP AS NEEDED)

- Get in sit-up position with your arms bent holding a dumbbell or powerblock on your chest even with your shoulders.
- Do a sit-up, touching your elbows to your thighs and then going back down.

SKULL CRUSHERS
12 REPS

- Lie on a bench with your knees bent and feet flat on the floor.
- Hold a barbell above your chest with your arms straight and your palms out.
- Bend your arms at the elbow until the barbell touches your forehead and then straighten to the start position.

METABOLIC

TRICEPS EXTENSION
THREE SETS OF 40 SECONDS

- Stand with your feet shoulder-width apart. Wrap a band around a pull-up bar or the top of a jungle gym and hold the ends in front of your face with your elbows at your sides.
- Push your hands down to your thighs, keeping your elbows in place, then come back to start.
- Do as many as possible in the allotted time.

FRIDAY

DAILY WARM-UP

- Refer to page 14.

MOVEMENT SERIES

POSITION SPECIFIC

- This series of the program is an opportunity for you as an athlete to choose your own exercises to work on your specific position(s). For example, if you are a wide receiver, work on your route tree; if you are a defensive back, work on press coverage; if you are a defensive end, work on leverage and getting off the ball. This workout can be as long as you feel it needs to be. Our suggestion is no more than an hour long, and be sure to warm up properly before any workout.

CORE SERIES

PAD PUNCHES
20 REPS EACH POSITION

POSITION 1

- Get into a sit-up position and have your partner hold an Airex pad even with your left hip and at a height so the middle of the pad is about shoulder height at the top of a sit-up. Do a sit-up, turn left and hit the pad with an open right hand.

POSITION 2

- Have your partner move to your right side.
- Do a sit-up, turn right and hit the pad with an open left hand.

(continued)

POSITION 3

- Have your partner stand at your feet.
- Do a sit-up and hit the pad with both open hands.

BLOCK 1 (FOUR CIRCUITS)

BARBELL HIGH PULL, SNATCH, ROW, FORWARD LUNGE
5 REPS

- Stand with your legs shoulder-width apart, holding a barbell with your palms facing your body.
- Bend your knees slightly and then bend your elbows to lift the bar to your chest in a high pull. Do this twice.
- With the same motion as the high pull, lift the bar over your head twice.
- Bend your knees about 45 degrees and bend your waist, pushing your butt back, lean forward and row the bar twice, bending your elbows and pulling the bar into your body.
- Stand straight and place the bar behind your neck on your shoulders with your palms out and do a forward lunge, first stepping forward with your right leg, then back to the start position and then step forward with left leg.

WEIGHTED PULL-UPS
10 REPS

- Hold a pull-up bar with a neutral grip.
- Bend your knees to 90 degrees, keep your legs together and hold a dead ball between your legs or rest it on your thighs.
- Do pull-ups.

DUMBBELL PUSH-UP TO ROW
8 REPS

- Get in push-up position with your hands on the dumbbells.
- Do a full push-up, down and up.
- Bend your right arm up until the dumbbell is even with your ribs.
- Straighten your arm back down to the ground.
- Bend your left arm up until the dumbbell is even with your ribs.
- Straighten your arm back to the ground.

PLATE SHRUGS
30 SECONDS

- Stand straight with your feet slightly apart.
- Hold a plate in each hand with your arms straight at your sides.
- Shrug your shoulders.

BLOCK 2 (THREE CIRCUITS)

VALSLIDE LATERAL LUNGE WITH EXTENSION
8 REPS ON EACH SIDE

- Put a Valslide under your left foot. For more of a challenge, hold a dead ball at your chest.
- Standing straight with your legs together, slide your left foot straight out to the side, bending your right knee and extending your right arm straight and across your body at shoulder height.

KETTLEBELL PUSH/PULL
10 REPS EACH SIDE

- Lie on a bench with a kettlebell in your right hand, elbow bent and the kettlebell at your shoulder.
- Hold the handle of a TRX band hanging from the jungle gym in your left hand with your palm toward your feet.
- Straighten your right arm, pushing the kettlebell toward the ceiling while pulling the band down to your body, twisting your hand 90 degrees so your palm is facing your body at the lowest point.

HEAVY PULL SLED
25 YARDS

- Pull a sled for 25 yards.

WEIGHTED PLANK
30 SECONDS

- Get into plank position.
- Have your partner put a plate on your lower back.
- Hold the position for the allotted time.

BLOCK 3 (THREE CIRCUITS)

SINGLE-LEGGED SQUAT
8 REPS EACH LEG

- Stand with one foot on a plyo box and the other foot suspended in the air, and hold small counter weights in your hand.
- Squat slowly on the leg that is on the box. Use the counter weights to extend your arms in front of you.
- Go as low as you can and then straighten up.

BACK FOOT ELEVATED DEAD BALL ROTATIONAL CHOP
10 REPS EACH SIDE

- Get in the forward lunge position with your left leg forward and right leg back on a plyo box balanced on your toes.
- Keeping your arms straight, lift a dead ball with both hands across your body to above your left shoulder.
- Bring your straight arms diagonally across your body in a chopping motion and throw the dead ball to the ground.

BATTLE ROPES
30 SECONDS

CHOOSE ONE OF THREE POSSIBILITIES

- Two-handed chops: Make chopping motions while holding the battle ropes, alternating your hands to make waves.

- Slams: Pick up and slam down the battle ropes with both hands.

(continued)

- Wave lunges: Do two-handed chops while doing forward lunges.

90-DEGREE PULL-UP HOLD
30 SECONDS

- Hold a pull-up bar with a neutral grip and your palms facing each other.
- Pull yourself up until your elbows are bent at 90 degrees.
- Hold for 30 seconds.

METABOLIC

SUPINE BICEPS
THREE SETS OF 40 SECONDS

- Lie on your back on a bench with your feet flat on the ground.
- Hold a dumbbell in each hand with your arms extended straight toward the ground below the bench.
- Bend your elbows and curl the dumbbells to your body height and then back down.
- Do as many as possible in the allotted time.

EXERCISE CHECKLIST

DAILY WARM UP – 14

CORRECTIVES
- ❏ Foam Roller
- ❏ Ankle Mobility with Band
- ❏ Knee Mobility
- ❏ Hip Mobility
- ❏ Thoracic Mobility
- ❏ Shoulder Mobility
- ❏ Glute Activation
- ❏ Monster Walk Steps

MOVEMENT
- ❏ A Skip
- ❏ B Skip
- ❏ Butt Kickers
- ❏ Quick Feet
- ❏ Falling Start

WEEK 1 – 18
MONDAY – 19

- ❏ Daily Warm-Up

MOVEMENT SERIES
- ❏ Suicide Shuffle

CORE SERIES
- ❏ Pillar Series—20 seconds each position

BLOCK 1 (THREE CIRCUITS)
- ❏ Barbell High Pull—8 reps
- ❏ Barbell Step-Up—5 reps each side
- ❏ Drop Squat to Box Jump—5 reps
- ❏ Ab Rollout—10 reps

BLOCK 2 (THREE CIRCUITS)
- ❏ Incline Bench (135 pounds)—10 reps
- ❏ Band Push-Up—20 reps
- ❏ Ipsilateral Kettlebell Romanian Dead Lift—8 reps
- ❏ Leg Raises—15 reps

BLOCK 3 (TWO CIRCUITS)
- ❏ Base Position Extension—8 reps
- ❏ Heavy Dumbbell Row 1¼—10 reps each arm
- ❏ Rotation Overhead Medicine Ball Slam—5 reps
- ❏ X Pull Down—10 reps

TUESDAY – 23

- ❏ Daily Warm-Up

MOVEMENT SERIES
- ❏ Single-Legged Hurdles—3 reps each leg
- ❏ Box Drill with Cones
- ❏ Lateral Ladder

CORE SERIES
- ❏ Push-Up Scapular Pillar Series—20 seconds, 10 seconds

BLOCK 1 (THREE CIRCUITS)
- ❏ Romanian Dead Lift to Power Shrug—5 reps
- ❏ Barbell Band Bench—8 reps (first circuit), 6 reps (second), 4 reps (third)
- ❏ Dumbbell Push-Up to Row—5 reps
- ❏ Valslide Hip Flexor Abs—8 reps each leg

BLOCK 2 (THREE CIRCUITS)
- ❏ Rear Foot Elevated Barbell Band Split Squat—5 reps each side
- ❏ Quad Hip Flexor Stretch—6 reps each side
- ❏ Ipsilateral Kettlebell Row—8 reps each side
- ❏ Face Pull—15 reps

BLOCK 3 (TWO CIRCUITS)
- ❏ Single-Legged Squat—8 reps each leg
- ❏ Squat to Truck Driver—6 reps
- ❏ Split-Stance Medicine Ball Overhead Slams—5 reps each side
- ❏ Half-Knee Curl Press—5 reps each leg

WEDNESDAY – 28

- ❏ Daily Warm-Up
- ❏ Recovery

THURSDAY – 29

- ❏ Daily Warm-Up

MOVEMENT SERIES
- ❏ Suicide Shuffle

CORE SERIES
- ❏ Abdominal Medicine Ball Throws—10 reps each position

BLOCK 1 (THREE CIRCUITS)
- ❏ Dumbbell Snatch—5 reps each arm
- ❏ Barbell Band Bench—15 seconds (first circuit), 10 seconds (second), 8 seconds (third)
- ❏ Medicine Ball Wall Chest Throws—10 reps
- ❏ Medicine Ball Overhead Throws—10 reps

BLOCK 2 (THREE CIRCUITS)
- ❏ Barbell Band Jump Squat—5 reps (first circuit), 7 reps (second), 9 reps (third)
- ❏ Medicine Ball Squat Wall Throw—5 reps
- ❏ Incline Dumbbell Row—8 reps
- ❏ Body Saw—10 reps

BLOCK 3 (TWO CIRCUITS)
- ❏ Split-Stance Medicine Ball Wall Throw—10 reps
- ❏ Lateral Lunge with Curl—5 reps
- ❏ Dips—10 reps
- ❏ EGG Cradles—10 reps

FRIDAY – 35

- ❏ Daily Warm-Up

MOVEMENT SERIES
- ❏ Single-Legged Hurdles—3 reps each leg
- ❏ Box Drill with Cones
- ❏ Lateral Single-Legged Ladders

CORE SERIES
- ❏ Pad Punches—10 reps each position

BLOCK 1 (THREE CIRCUITS)
- ❏ Hang Clean/Front Squat/Overhead Press—3 reps
- ❏ Trap Bar—6 reps (first circuit), 5 reps (second), 4 reps (third)
- ❏ Quad Hip Flexor Stretch—6 reps each side
- ❏ Heavy Weighted Abs—15 reps (start at 35 pounds and go up as needed)

BLOCK 2 (THREE CIRCUITS)
- ❏ Valslide Lunge—6 reps each side
- ❏ Incline Band Bench—5 reps
- ❏ Eccentric Neutral Grip Pull-Ups—5 reps
- ❏ Battle Ropes—30 seconds

BLOCK 3 (TWO CIRCUITS)
- ❏ Dumbbell Bench 1½—20 seconds
- ❏ Dumbbell Row 1½—20 seconds each arm
- ❏ Bicep Curl—20 seconds
- ❏ Triceps Push Down—20 seconds

WEEK 2 - 41
MONDAY - 42

- ❏ Daily Warm-Up

MOVEMENT SERIES
- ❏ Suicide Shuttle

CORE SERIES
- ❏ Pillar Series—20 seconds each position

BLOCK 1 (THREE CIRCUITS)
- ❏ Barbell High Pull—8 reps
- ❏ Front Foot Elevated Valslide Lunge—
  8 reps each side
- ❏ Quad Hip Flexor Stretch—6 reps each side
- ❏ Plate Sit-Ups—15 reps

BLOCK 2 (THREE CIRCUITS)
- ❏ Eccentric Neutral Grip Pull-Ups—8 reps
- ❏ Partner Band Row—10 reps each arm
- ❏ Single-Legged Squat—8 reps each leg
- ❏ Valslide Hip Flexor Abs—8 reps each leg

BLOCK 3 (TWO CIRCUITS)
- ❏ Dumbbell Broad Jump—5 reps
- ❏ Wide-Legged Seated Kettlebell Rotational
  Press—8 reps
- ❏ Split-Stance Medicine Overhead Ball Slams—
  5 reps each side
- ❏ Leg Throws—10 reps

TUESDAY - 47

- ❏ Daily Warm-Up

MOVEMENT SERIES
- ❏ Double-Legged Hurdles—3 reps
- ❏ 3 Cone Drill
- ❏ Lateral Double-Legged Ladders

CORE SERIES
- ❏ Push-Up Scapular Pillar Series—20 seconds,
  10 seconds

BLOCK 1 (THREE CIRCUITS)
- ❏ Barbell Clean to Press—5 reps
- ❏ Dumbbell Bench Hips Off—8 reps
- ❏ Plate Push-Up—10 reps
- ❏ Leg Raises—15 reps

BLOCK 2 (THREE CIRCUITS)
- ❏ Lateral Valslide Lunge—8 reps each side
- ❏ Adductor Stretch—6 reps
- ❏ Dumbbell Push-Up to Row—5 reps
- ❏ Plate Holds—30 seconds

BLOCK 3 (TWO CIRCUITS)
- ❏ Lateral Rotation Box Jumps—3 reps each side
- ❏ Band Rotation Pull/Chop—10 reps each side
- ❏ Reverse Medicine Ball Wall Throw—5 reps
- ❏ Valslide Runners—20 seconds

WEDNESDAY - 52

- ❏ Daily Warm-Up
- ❏ Recovery

THURSDAY - 53

- ❏ Daily Warm-Up

MOVEMENT SERIES
- ❏ 300-Yard Shuttle Run

CORE SERIES
- ❏ Seated Medicine Ball Throws—Three sets of
  15 reps

BLOCK 1 (THREE CIRCUITS)
- ❏ Kettlebell Swing—10 reps
- ❏ Kettlebell Squat to Press—10 reps
- ❏ Push Sled—25 yards
- ❏ Quad Hip Flexor Stretch—6 reps each side

BLOCK 2 (THREE CIRCUITS)
- ❏ Dumbbell Incline Bench Reverse Flies—12 reps
- ❏ Bulgarian Squat—8 reps each side
- ❏ Treadmill Push—20 seconds
- ❏ Medicine Ball Double Crunch—15 reps

BLOCK 3 (TWO CIRCUITS)
- ❏ Dead Ball Explosive Wall Throws—3 reps
  each side
- ❏ Shoulder 30s—10 reps each position
- ❏ Stability Ball Hamstring Curls—12 reps
- ❏ Stability Ball Planks—20 seconds

FRIDAY - 58

- ❏ Daily Warm-Up

MOVEMENT SERIES
- ❏ Double-Legged Hurdles—3 reps
- ❏ 3 Cone Drill
- ❏ Lateral Double-Legged Ladders

CORE SERIES
- ❏ Pad Punches—10 reps each position

BLOCK 1 (THREE CIRCUITS)
- ❏ Band Squat—20 seconds
- ❏ Bike—20 seconds
- ❏ Barbell Band Bench—20 seconds
- ❏ Band Row—20 seconds

BLOCK 2 (THREE CIRCUITS)
- ❏ Band Squat to Wrap—20 seconds
- ❏ Band High Pull—20 seconds
- ❏ Band Bi (Bicep Curls with Band)—20 seconds
- ❏ Band Tri—20 seconds

BLOCK 3 (TWO CIRCUITS)
- ❏ Battle Ropes—20 seconds
- ❏ V-Ups—20 seconds
- ❏ Planks—20 seconds

WEEK 3 - 64
MONDAY - 65

- ❏ Daily Warm-Up

MOVEMENT SERIES
- ❏ 300-Yard Shuttle Run

CORE SERIES
- ❏ Pillar Series—20 seconds each position

BLOCK 1 (THREE CIRCUITS)
- ❏ Two-Arm Kettlebell High Pull Clean and Squat to
  Press Series—3 reps
- ❏ Kettlebell Goblet Squat Holds—20 seconds
- ❏ Band Resistant Lunge—3 reps
- ❏ Heavy Weighted Abs—15 reps (start at 35
  pounds and go up as needed)

BLOCK 2 (THREE CIRCUITS)
- ❏ Incline Band Bench—8 reps
- ❏ Standing Ts—6 reps each leg
- ❏ Dead Ball Squat to Wall Throw—5 reps
- ❏ EGG Cradles—12 reps

BLOCK 3 (TWO CIRCUITS)
- ❏ Box Jump Two to One—3 reps each side
- ❏ Reactive Medicine Ball Wall Throw—5 reps
  each side
- ❏ Oblique Band Rotation—10 reps each way
- ❏ Farmer's Walk—50 yards

TUESDAY - 69

- ❏ Daily Warm-Up

MOVEMENT SERIES
- ❏ Single- and Double-Legged Hurdles—3 reps
- ❏ L Drill with Cones
- ❏ Icky Shuffle Ladders

CORE SERIES
- ❏ Push-Up Scapular Pillar Series—20 seconds,
  10 seconds

BLOCK 1 (THREE CIRCUITS)
- [ ] Single-Arm Dumbbell Snatch to Press—5 reps each arm
- [ ] Rope Sled Pull—25 yards
- [ ] Heavy Dumbbell Row—5 reps
- [ ] Lateral Stretch—6 reps

BLOCK 2 (THREE CIRCUITS)
- [ ] Dumbbell Pullover—10 reps
- [ ] Squat to Truck Driver—8 reps
- [ ] Dumbbell Side Bends—15 reps each side

BLOCK 3 (TWO CIRCUITS)
- [ ] Dumbbell Push-Up to Row—5 reps
- [ ] Band Row—20 seconds
- [ ] Medicine Ball Parallel Wall Throw—10 reps
- [ ] Plank Walks—25 yards

WEDNESDAY – 73
- [ ] Daily Warm-Up
- [ ] Recovery

THURSDAY – 76
- [ ] Daily Warm-Up

MOVEMENT SERIES
- [ ] 300-Yard Shuttle Run

CORE SERIES
- [ ] Seated Medicine Ball Throws—10 reps

BLOCK 1 (THREE CIRCUITS)
- [ ] RDL to High Pull—8 reps
- [ ] Band Squat—8 reps
- [ ] Sumo Squat to Hamstring Stretch—6 reps
- [ ] Snatch Grip Abs—15 reps

BLOCK 2 (THREE CIRCUITS)
- [ ] Incline Alternating Dumbbell Bench—8 reps
- [ ] Pad Push-Up—10 reps
- [ ] Stability Ball Hamstring Curls—8 reps
- [ ] Body Saw—12 reps

BLOCK 3 (TWO CIRCUITS)
- [ ] Lateral Rotation Box Jumps—3 reps each side
- [ ] Dead Ball Squat to Wall Throw—5 reps
- [ ] Wide-Legged Seated Kettlebell Rotational Press—8 reps
- [ ] Valslide Pikes—15 reps

FRIDAY – 80
- [ ] Daily Warm-Up

MOVEMENT SERIES
- [ ] Single- and Double-Legged Hurdles—3 reps
- [ ] L Drill with Cones
- [ ] Icky Shuffle Ladders

CORE SERIES
- [ ] Pad Punches—10 reps each position

BLOCK 1 (THREE CIRCUITS)
- [ ] Barbell Clean, Forward Lunge to Press—3 reps
- [ ] Dumbbell Bench Single, Single, Double—5 reps
- [ ] Face Pull—15 rep
- [ ] Double Crunch—15 reps

BLOCK 2 (THREE CIRCUITS)
- [ ] Lateral Lunge to Press—8 reps each leg
- [ ] Adductor Stretch—6 reps
- [ ] Jungle Gym (or TRX) Push-Up—12 reps
- [ ] Medicine Ball Plank Holds—20 seconds

BLOCK 3 (TWO CIRCUITS)
- [ ] Medicine Ball Wall Chest Throws—20 seconds
- [ ] Jungle Gym (or TRX Band) Reverse Flies—10 reps
- [ ] Medicine Ball Perpendicular Wall Throw—10 reps each side
- [ ] Sit-Up to Rotational Press—8 reps

WEEK 4 – 86
MONDAY – 87
- [ ] Daily Warm-Up

MOVEMENT SERIES
- [ ] 300-Yard Shuttle Run

CORE SERIES
- [ ] Pillar Series—20 seconds each position

BLOCK 1 (THREE CIRCUITS)
- [ ] 3-Position Clean—3 reps
- [ ] Kettlebell Offset Front Squat—8 reps each side
- [ ] Bike—20 seconds
- [ ] Quad Hip Flexor Stretch—6 reps each side

BLOCK 2 (THREE CIRCUITS)
- [ ] Walking Lunge with Rotation—5 reps
- [ ] Barbell Band Bench—5 reps
- [ ] Shoulder Taps—20 seconds
- [ ] Split-Stance Dead Ball Rotational Chop—5 reps each side

BLOCK 3 (TWO CIRCUITS)
- [ ] Glute Bridge—20 seconds
- [ ] Jungle Gym (or TRX) Hamstring Curls 1½—5 reps
- [ ] Push-Up with Reach—8 reps each arm

TUESDAY – 91
- [ ] Daily Warm-Up

MOVEMENT SERIES
- [ ] Single- and Double-Legged Hurdles—3 reps
- [ ] Box Drill with Cones
- [ ] Skier's Ladder

CORE SERIES
- [ ] Push-Up Scapular Pillar Series—20 seconds, 10 seconds

BLOCK 1 (THREE CIRCUITS)
- [ ] Single-Arm Dumbbell Snatch to Press—4 reps each arm
- [ ] Contralateral Row—8 reps each side
- [ ] Single-Arm Alternating Kettlebell Swing—8 reps
- [ ] Band Jump—5 reps

BLOCK 2 (THREE CIRCUITS)
- [ ] Dead Ball Transverse Lateral Step-Up—8 reps each side
- [ ] Medicine Ball Push-Up—5 reps
- [ ] Single-Legged Medicine Ball Slams—8 reps each leg
- [ ] Jungle Gym (or TRX) Marches—10 reps

BLOCK 3 (TWO CIRCUITS)
- [ ] Closed Grip Band Bench—20 seconds
- [ ] Shoulder 30s—10 reps each position
- [ ] Lateral Lunge—8 reps
- [ ] Push Plate—25 yards

WEDNESDAY – 97
- [ ] Daily Warm-Up
- [ ] Recovery

THURSDAY – 100
- [ ] Daily Warm-Up

MOVEMENT SERIES
- [ ] 300-Yard Shuttle Run

CORE SERIES
- [ ] Seated Medicine Ball Throws—10 reps

BLOCK 1 (THREE CIRCUITS)
- [ ] Dumbbell Squat to Jump—5 reps
- [ ] Dumbbell Reverse Lunge to Knee Drive—8 reps each leg
- [ ] Quad Hip Flexor Stretch—6 reps
- [ ] Resisted Run—20 seconds

BLOCK 2 (THREE CIRCUITS)
- ❑ Dumbbell Slide Reach to Row—5 reps each arm
- ❑ Three-Way Push-Up—5 reps
- ❑ Front Plank with Row—10 reps each arm
- ❑ Battle Ropes—20 seconds

BLOCK 3 (TWO CIRCUITS)
- ❑ Single-Legged Squat with Medicine Ball Extension—8 reps
- ❑ Barbell Curl 1½—10 reps
- ❑ Resisted Backpedal—10 to 15 yards
- ❑ X Pull Down—15 reps

FRIDAY – 105
- ❑ Daily Warm-Up

MOVEMENT SERIES
- ❑ Single- and Double-Legged Hurdles—3 reps
- ❑ Box Drill with Cones
- ❑ Skier's Ladder

CORE SERIES
- ❑ Pad Punches—10 reps each position

BLOCK 1 (THREE CIRCUITS)
- ❑ Snatch Grip High Pull—5 reps
- ❑ Jungle Gym Weighted Row—10 reps
- ❑ Snatch Grip Abs—15 reps
- ❑ Pretzel Stretch—6 reps each side

BLOCK 2 (THREE CIRCUITS)
- ❑ Front Foot Elevated Split-Stance Row—10 reps each side
- ❑ Kettlebell Push/Pull—10 reps each arm
- ❑ Single-Legged Barbell RDL—8 reps on each leg
- ❑ Plank with Rotation—8 reps

BLOCK 3 (TWO CIRCUITS)
- ❑ Dumbbell Bench 1½—20 seconds
- ❑ Dumbbell Row—20 seconds each arm
- ❑ Triceps Kickback—20 seconds
- ❑ Supine Bicep Curls—20 seconds

WEEK 5 – 111
MONDAY – 112
- ❑ Daily Warm-Up

MOVEMENT SERIES
- ❑ Suicide Shuffle

CORE SERIES
- ❑ Pillar Series—25 seconds each position

BLOCK 1 (THREE CIRCUITS)
- ❑ Dumbbell High Pull—8 reps
- ❑ Dumbbell Step-Ups—8 reps each leg
- ❑ Medicine Ball Squat Throws—5 reps
- ❑ Heavy Weighted Abs—15 reps (start at 35 pounds and go up as needed)

BLOCK 2 (THREE CIRCUITS)
- ❑ Incline Dumbbell Bench Press (135 pounds)—10 reps
- ❑ Medicine Ball Push-Up—15 reps
- ❑ Ipsilateral Dumbbell RDL—8 reps
- ❑ Weighted Leg Raises—15 reps

BLOCK 3 (TWO CIRCUITS)
- ❑ Medicine Ball RDL Wall Throw—6 reps each leg
- ❑ Heavy Dumbbell Row 1½—8 reps each arm
- ❑ Band Rotation Pull/Chop—8 reps each side
- ❑ Plank Row—10 reps each arm

METABOLIC
- ❑ Battle Ropes—Three sets of 30 seconds

TUESDAY – 116
- ❑ Daily Warm-Up

MOVEMENT SERIES
- ❑ Sled Sprint—50 yards
- ❑ 3 Cone Drill
- ❑ Lateral Single-Legged Ladders

CORE SERIES
- ❑ Push-Up Scapular Pillar Series—25 seconds, 15 seconds each position

BLOCK 1 (THREE CIRCUITS)
- ❑ Dumbbell RDL to Shrug—5 reps
- ❑ Alternate Dumbbell Bench—8 reps
- ❑ Dumbbell Push-Up to Row—6 reps

BLOCK 2 (THREE CIRCUITS)
- ❑ Rear Foot Elevated Barbell Band Split Squat—6 reps each side
- ❑ Quad Hip Flexor Stretch—6 reps each side
- ❑ Contralateral Row—8 reps each side
- ❑ Dumbbell Reverse Flies—10 reps

BLOCK 3 (THREE CIRCUITS)
- ❑ Single-Legged Squat—8 reps each leg
- ❑ Squat to Truck Driver—8 reps
- ❑ Split-Stance Medicine Ball Overhead Slams—5 reps each side
- ❑ Half-Knee Curl Press—10 reps each leg forward

METABOLIC
- ❑ Band Bi (Bicep Curls with Band)—Three sets of 30 seconds

WEDNESDAY – 124
- ❑ Daily Warm-Up
- ❑ Recovery

THURSDAY – 124
- ❑ Daily Warm-Up

MOVEMENT SERIES
- ❑ Suicide Shuffle

CORE SERIES
- ❑ Seated Medicine Ball Throws—15 reps

BLOCK 1 (THREE CIRCUITS)
- ❑ Single-Arm Dumbbell Snatch—5 reps each arm
- ❑ Dumbbell Bench—10 reps
- ❑ Weighted Pull-Ups—8 reps
- ❑ Planks—25 seconds

BLOCK 2 (THREE CIRCUITS)
- ❑ Dumbbell Squat to Jump—5 reps
- ❑ Medicine Ball Parallel Wall Throw—5 reps
- ❑ Incline Dumbbell Row—8 reps
- ❑ Body Saw—10 reps

BLOCK 3 (THREE CIRCUITS)
- ❑ Box Jump Two to One—3 reps each side
- ❑ Reactive Medicine Ball Wall Throw—5 reps each side
- ❑ Oblique Band Rotation—10 reps each side
- ❑ Farmer's Walk—50 yards

METABOLIC
- ❑ Incline Band Flies—Three sets of 30 seconds

FRIDAY – 129
- ❑ Daily Warm-Up

MOVEMENT SERIES
- ❑ Sled Sprint—50 yards
- ❑ L Drill with Cones
- ❑ Lateral Single-Legged Ladders

CORE SERIES
- ❑ Pad Punches—15 reps each position

BLOCK 1 (THREE CIRCUITS)
- ❑ Dumbbell Hang Clean and Front Squat—4 reps
- ❑ Trap Bar—8 reps (first circuit), 6 reps (second), 4 reps (third)
- ❑ Pretzel Stretch—6 reps each side
- ❑ Russian Twist—6 reps

BLOCK 2 (THREE CIRCUITS)
- ❏ Lunge Twists—6 reps each leg
- ❏ Incline Dumbbell Bench Press (135 pounds)—8 reps
- ❏ Eccentric Neutral Grip Pull-Ups—5 reps
- ❏ Battle Ropes—25 seconds

BLOCK 3 (THREE CIRCUITS)
- ❏ Dumbbell Push-Up to Row—5 reps
- ❏ Band Row—25 seconds
- ❏ Medicine Ball Parallel Wall Throw—10 reps
- ❏ Plank Walks—25 yards

METABOLIC
- ❏ Band Row—Three sets of 30 seconds

WEEK 6 – 135
MONDAY – 136

- ❏ Daily Warm-Up

MOVEMENT SERIES
- ❏ 300-Yard Shuttle Run

CORE SERIES
- ❏ Pillar Series—25 seconds each position

BLOCK 1 (THREE CIRCUITS)
- ❏ 3-Position Clean—3 reps
- ❏ Kettlebell Offset Front Squat—8 reps each side
- ❏ Bike—25 seconds
- ❏ Quad Hip Flexor Stretch—6 reps each side

BLOCK 2 (THREE CIRCUITS)
- ❏ Walking Lunge with Rotation—5 reps
- ❏ Barbell Band Bench—5 reps
- ❏ Shoulder Taps—25 seconds
- ❏ Split-Stance Dead Ball Rotational Chop—5 reps each side

BLOCK 3 (THREE CIRCUITS)
- ❏ Glute Bridge—25 seconds
- ❏ Jungle Gym (or TRX) Hamstring Curls 1½—5 reps
- ❏ Leg Lowering Hamstring Stretch—6 reps each leg
- ❏ Push-Up with Reach—8 reps each arm

METABOLIC
- ❏ Battle Ropes—Three sets of 30 seconds

TUESDAY – 142

- ❏ Daily Warm-Up

MOVEMENT SERIES
- ❏ Kneeling Sprints—25 yards max, 5 times each knee
- ❏ L Drill with Cones
- ❏ Lateral Double-Legged Ladders

CORE SERIES
- ❏ Push-Up Scapular Pillar Series—25 seconds, 15 seconds each position

BLOCK 1 (THREE CIRCUITS)
- ❏ Single-Arm Dumbbell Snatch to Press—4 reps each arm
- ❏ Contralateral Row—8 reps each side
- ❏ Single-Arm Alternating Kettlebell Swing—8 reps
- ❏ Band Jump—5 reps

BLOCK 2 (THREE CIRCUITS)
- ❏ Transverse Step-Up Medicine Ball Push—8 reps each side
- ❏ Medicine Ball Push-Up—5 reps
- ❏ Single-Legged Medicine Ball Slams—8 reps each leg
- ❏ Jungle Gym (or TRX) Marches—10 reps

BLOCK 3 (THREE CIRCUITS)
- ❏ Closed Grip Band Bench—25 seconds
- ❏ Shoulder 30s—10 reps each position
- ❏ Lateral Lunge—8 reps
- ❏ Push Plate—25 yards

METABOLIC
- ❏ Band Tri—Three sets of 30 seconds

WEDNESDAY – 147

- ❏ Daily Warm-Up
- ❏ Recovery

THURSDAY – 150

- ❏ Daily Warm-Up

MOVEMENT SERIES
- ❏ 300-Yard Shuttle Run

CORE SERIES
- ❏ Seated Medicine Ball Throws—Three sets of 15 reps

BLOCK 1 (THREE CIRCUITS)
- ❏ Dumbbell Squat to Jump—5 reps
- ❏ Dumbbell Reverse Lunge to Knee Drive—8 reps each leg
- ❏ Quad Hip Flexor Stretch—6 reps each side
- ❏ Resisted Run—25 seconds

BLOCK 2 (THREE CIRCUITS)
- ❏ Dumbbell Slide Reach to Row—5 reps each arm
- ❏ Three-Way Push-Up—5 reps
- ❏ Front Plank with Row—10 reps each arm
- ❏ Battle Ropes—25 seconds

BLOCK 3 (THREE CIRCUITS)
- ❏ Dumbbell Bench 1½—25 seconds
- ❏ Dumbbell Row—25 seconds each arm
- ❏ Triceps Kickback—25 seconds
- ❏ Supine Bicep Curls—25 seconds

METABOLIC
- ❏ Band Squat to Wrap—3 sets of reps of 30 seconds

FRIDAY – 155

- ❏ Daily Warm-Up

MOVEMENT SERIES
- ❏ Kneeling Sprints—25 yards max, 5 times each knee
- ❏ L Drill with Cones
- ❏ Lateral Double-Legged Ladders

CORE SERIES
- ❏ Pad Punches—15 reps each position

BLOCK 1 (THREE CIRCUITS)
- ❏ Snatch Grip High Pull—5 reps
- ❏ Jungle Gym Weighted Row—10 reps
- ❏ Snatch Grip Abs—15 reps
- ❏ Pretzel Stretch—6 reps on each side

BLOCK 2 (THREE CIRCUITS)
- ❏ Front Foot Elevated Split-Stance Row—10 reps each side
- ❏ Single-Legged Barbell RDL—8 reps each leg
- ❏ Plank with Rotation—8 reps

BLOCK 3 (THREE CIRCUITS)
- ❏ Dumbbell Bench 1½—25 seconds
- ❏ Dumbbell Row—25 seconds each side
- ❏ Triceps Kickback—25 seconds
- ❏ Supine Bicep Curls—25 seconds

METABOLIC
- ❏ Band Squat to Wrap—3 sets of reps of 30 seconds

WEEK 7 – 161
MONDAY – 162

❑ Daily Warm-Up

MOVEMENT SERIES
❑ Suicide Shuffle

CORE SERIES
❑ Pillar Series—25 seconds each position

BLOCK 1 (THREE CIRCUITS)
❑ Barbell High Pull—8 reps
❑ Front Foot Elevated Valslide Lunge—8 reps each side
❑ Quad Hip Flexor Stretch—6 reps each side
❑ Plate Sit-Ups—15 reps

BLOCK 2 (THREE CIRCUITS)
❑ Eccentric Neutral Grip Pull-Ups—8 reps
❑ Partner Band Row—10 reps each arm
❑ Single-Legged Squat—8 reps each leg
❑ Valslide Hip Flexor Abs—8 reps each side

BLOCK 3 (THREE CIRCUITS)
❑ Dead Ball Broad Jump—5 reps
❑ Wide-Legged Seated Kettlebell Rotational Press—8 reps
❑ Split-Stance Medicine Ball Overhead Slams—5 reps each side
❑ Leg Throws—15 reps

METABOLIC
❑ Supine Biceps—Three sets of 30 seconds

TUESDAY – 167

❑ Daily Warm-Up

MOVEMENT SERIES
❑ Single- and Double-Legged Hurdles
❑ L Drill with Cones
❑ Icky Shuffle Ladders

CORE SERIES
❑ Push-Up Scapular Pillar Series—25 seconds, 15 seconds each position

BLOCK 1 (THREE CIRCUITS)
❑ Barbell Clean to Press—5 reps
❑ Dumbbell Bench Hips Off—8 reps
❑ Plate Push-Up—10 reps
❑ Leg Raises—15 reps

BLOCK 2 (THREE CIRCUITS)
❑ Lateral Valslide Lunge—8 reps
❑ Adductor Stretch—6 reps
❑ Dumbbell Push-Up to Row—5 reps
❑ Plate Holds—25 seconds

BLOCK 3 (THREE CIRCUITS)
❑ Lateral Rotation Box Jumps—3 reps each side
❑ Band Rotation Pull/Chop—10 reps each side
❑ Reverse Medicine Ball Wall Throw—5 reps
❑ Valslide Runners—25 seconds

METABOLIC
❑ Treadmill Sprints—Three sets of 30 seconds

WEDNESDAY – 172

❑ Daily Warm-Up
❑ Recovery

THURSDAY – 172

❑ Daily Warm-Up

MOVEMENT SERIES
❑ Suicide Shuffle

CORE SERIES
❑ Seated Medicine Ball Throws—Three sets of 15 reps

BLOCK 1 (THREE CIRCUITS)
❑ Kettlebell Swing—10 reps
❑ Kettlebell Squat to Press—10 reps
❑ Push Sled—25 yards
❑ Quad Hip Flexor Stretch—6 reps on each side

BLOCK 2 (THREE CIRCUITS)
❑ Dumbbell Incline Bench Reverse Flies—12 reps
❑ Bulgarian Squat—8 reps each side
❑ Treadmill Push—25 seconds
❑ Medicine Ball Double Crunch—15 reps

BLOCK 3 (THREE CIRCUITS)
❑ Dead Ball Explosive Wall Throw—3 reps each side
❑ Shoulder 30s—10 reps each position
❑ Stability Ball Hamstring Curls—12 reps
❑ Stability Ball Planks—25 seconds

METABOLIC
❑ Battle Ropes—Three sets of 30 seconds

FRIDAY – 179

❑ Daily Warm-Up

MOVEMENT SERIES
❑ Single- and Double-Legged Hurdles—3 reps
❑ L Drill with Cones
❑ Icky Shuffle Ladders

CORE SERIES
❑ Pad Punches—15 reps each position

BLOCK 1 (THREE CIRCUITS)
❑ Band Squat—25 seconds
❑ Bike—25 seconds
❑ Barbell Band Bench—25 seconds
❑ Band Row—25 seconds

BLOCK 2 (THREE CIRCUITS)
❑ Band Squat to Wrap—25 seconds
❑ Band High Pull—25 seconds
❑ Band Bi (Bicep Curls with Band)—25 seconds
❑ Band Tri—25 seconds

BLOCK 3 (THREE CIRCUITS)
❑ Battle Ropes—25 seconds
❑ V-Ups—25 seconds

METABOLIC
❑ Battle Ropes—Three sets of 30 seconds

WEEK 8 – 185
MONDAY – 186

❑ Daily Warm-Up

MOVEMENT SERIES
❑ Suicide Shuffle

CORE SERIES
❑ Pillar Series—25 seconds each position

BLOCK 1 (THREE CIRCUITS)
❑ 3-Position Clean—3 reps
❑ Kettlebell Offset Front Squat—8 reps each side
❑ Bike—25 seconds
❑ Quad Hip Flexor Stretch—6 reps each side

BLOCK 2 (THREE CIRCUITS)
❑ Incline Bench (135 Pounds) —10 reps
❑ Band Push-Ups—20 reps
❑ Ipsilateral Kettlebell Romanian Dead Lift—8 reps
❑ Leg Raises—15 reps

BLOCK 3 (THREE CIRCUITS)
❑ Box Jump Two to One—3 reps each side
❑ Reactive Medicine Ball Wall Throw—5 reps each side
❑ Oblique Band Rotation—10 reps each side
❑ Farmer's Walk—50 yards

METABOLIC
- ❏ Partner Plank—Three sets of 30 seconds

TUESDAY – 191
- ❏ Daily Warm-Up

MOVEMENT SERIES
- ❏ Single- and Double-Legged Hurdles—3 reps
- ❏ *L* Drill with Cones
- ❏ Icky Shuffle Ladders

CORE SERIES
- ❏ Push-Up Scapular Pillar Series—25 seconds, 15 seconds each position

BLOCK 1 (THREE CIRCUITS)
- ❏ Single-Arm Dumbbell Snatch to Press—4 reps each arm
- ❏ Contralateral Row—8 reps each side
- ❏ Single-Arm Alternating Kettlebell Swing—8 reps each side
- ❏ Band Jump—5 reps

BLOCK 2 (THREE CIRCUITS)
- ❏ Rear Foot Elevated Barbell Band Split Squat—5 reps each side
- ❏ Quad Hip Flexor Stretch—6 reps both sides
- ❏ Ipsilateral Kettlebell Row—8 reps each side
- ❏ Face Pull—15 reps

BLOCK 3 (THREE CIRCUITS)
- ❏ Dumbbell Push-Up to Row—5 reps
- ❏ Band Row—25 seconds
- ❏ Medicine Ball Parallel Wall Throw—10 reps
- ❏ Plank Walks—25 yards

METABOLIC
- ❏ Incline Band Flies—Three sets of 30 seconds

WEDNESDAY – 196
- ❏ Daily Warm-Up
- ❏ Recovery

THURSDAY – 197
- ❏ Daily Warm-Up

MOVEMENT SERIES
- ❏ Suicide Shuffle

CORE SERIES
- ❏ Seated Medicine Ball Throws—Three sets of 15 reps

BLOCK 1 (THREE CIRCUITS)
- ❏ Dumbbell Squat to Jump to Forward Lunge—5 reps each leg
- ❏ Dumbbell Reverse Lunge to Knee Drive—8 reps each side
- ❏ Quad Hip Flexor Stretch—6 reps each side
- ❏ Resisted Run—25 seconds

BLOCK 2 (THREE CIRCUITS)
- ❏ Barbell Band Jump Squats—5 reps
- ❏ Medicine Ball Squat Wall Throw—5 reps
- ❏ Incline Dumbbell Row—8 reps
- ❏ Body Saw—10 reps

BLOCK 3 (THREE CIRCUITS)
- ❏ Lateral Rotation Box Jumps—3 reps each side
- ❏ Dead Ball Squat to Throw—5 reps
- ❏ Wide-Legged Seated Kettlebell Rotational Press—8 reps
- ❏ Valslide Pikes—15 reps

METABOLIC
- ❏ Band Bi (Bicep Curls with Band—Three sets of 30 seconds

FRIDAY – 204
- ❏ Daily Warm-Up

MOVEMENT SERIES
- ❏ Single- and Double-Legged Hurdles—3 reps
- ❏ *L* Drill with Cones
- ❏ Icky Shuffle Ladders

CORE SERIES
- ❏ Pad Punches—15 reps each position

BLOCK 1 (THREE CIRCUITS)
- ❏ Snatch Grip High Pull—5 reps
- ❏ Jungle Gym Weighted Row—10 reps
- ❏ Snatch Grip Abs—15 reps
- ❏ Pretzel Stretch—6 reps each side

BLOCK 2 (THREE CIRCUITS)
- ❏ Valslide Lunge—6 reps
- ❏ Incline Band Bench—8 reps
- ❏ Eccentric Neutral Grip Pull-Ups—5 reps
- ❏ Battle Ropes—25 seconds

BLOCK 3 (THREE CIRCUITS)
- ❏ Medicine Ball Chest Pass—25 seconds
- ❏ Jungle Gym (or TRX Band) Reverse Flies—10 reps
- ❏ Medicine Ball Perpendicular Wall Throw—10 reps each side
- ❏ Kettlebell Sit-Up to Rotational Press—8 reps

METABOLIC
- ❏ Battle Ropes—Three sets of 30 seconds

WEEK 9 – 210
MONDAY – 211
- ❏ Daily Warm-Up

MOVEMENT SERIES
- ❏ Suicide Shuffle

CORE SERIES
- ❏ Pillar Series—30 seconds each position

BLOCK 1 (FOUR CIRCUITS)
- ❏ Dumbbell Clean to Armpit—8 reps
- ❏ Contralateral Valslide Lunge—8 reps each leg (first circuit), 6 reps (second), 5 reps (third), 4 reps (fourth)
- ❏ Quad Hip Flexor Stretch—6 reps each side
- ❏ Alternate Dumbbell Bench—8 reps each arm

BLOCK 2 (THREE CIRCUITS)
- ❏ Dumbbell Push-Up to Row—8 reps
- ❏ Medicine Ball Wall Chest Throws—30 seconds
- ❏ Sled Sprint—Maximum 25 yards, 2 reps
- ❏ Plank with Rotation—8 reps

BLOCK 3 (THREE CIRCUITS)
- ❏ Jungle Gym (or TRX) Single-Legged Hamstring Curls—5 reps each side
- ❏ Shoulder 30s—10 reps each position
- ❏ Wide-Legged Seated Kettlebell Rotational Press—8 reps
- ❏ X Pull Down—12 reps

METABOLIC
- ❏ Incline Band Flies—Three sets of 40 seconds

TUESDAY – 216
- ❏ Daily Warm-Up

MOVEMENT SERIES
- ❏ Sled Sprint—50 yards
- ❏ *L* Drill with Cones
- ❏ Lateral Single-Legged Ladders

CORE SERIES
- ❏ Push-Up Scapular Pillar Series—30 seconds, 20 seconds each position

BLOCK 1 (FOUR CIRCUITS)
- ❏ Single-Legged Barbell RDL to Power Shrug—8 reps each leg
- ❏ Glute Activation—10 reps each side, then 10 with both legs together
- ❏ Barbell Step-Up—8 reps each side (first circuit), 6 reps (second), 5 reps (third), 4 reps (fourth)
- ❏ Band Quad Hip Flexor Stretch—6 reps each leg

BLOCK 2 (THREE CIRCUITS)
- ❑ Eccentric Neutral Grip Pull-Ups—8 reps
- ❑ Partner Band Row—8 reps each arm
- ❑ Lateral Stretch—6 reps
- ❑ Reverse Medicine Ball Wall Throw—6 reps

BLOCK 3 (THREE CIRCUITS)
- ❑ Single-Legged Squat—8 reps each leg
- ❑ Dumbbell Slide Reach to Row—5 reps each arm
- ❑ Dumbbell Wood Chop—8 reps each side
- ❑ Barbell Curl 1½—10 reps

METABOLIC
- ❑ Band Pull Down—Three sets of 40 seconds

WEDNESDAY – 222
- ❑ Daily Warm-Up
- ❑ Recovery

THURSDAY – 222
- ❑ Daily Warm-Up

MOVEMENT SERIES
- ❑ Suicide Shuffle

CORE SERIES
- ❑ Seated Medicine Ball Throws—Three sets of 20 reps

BLOCK 1 (FOUR CIRCUITS)
- ❑ Single-Arm Dumbbell Snatch—5 reps each arm
- ❑ Incline Bench—10 reps (first circuit), 8 reps (second), 6 reps (third), 4 reps (fourth)
- ❑ Plate Push-Up—10 reps
- ❑ Heavy Weighted Abs—15 reps (start at 35 pounds and go up as needed)

BLOCK 2 (THREE CIRCUITS)
- ❑ Lunge with Rotation—8 reps
- ❑ Quad Hip Flexor Stretch—6 reps each side
- ❑ Bike—40 seconds
- ❑ Battle Ropes—30 seconds

BLOCK 3 (THREE CIRCUITS)
- ❑ Rotational Lift—8 reps each side
- ❑ Split-Stance Medicine Ball Overhead Slams—30 seconds
- ❑ Dumbbell Chest Fly—12 reps
- ❑ Dumbbell Shoulder Shrug—12 reps

METABOLIC
- ❑ Supine Bicep Curls—Three sets of 40 seconds

FRIDAY – 229
- ❑ Daily Warm-Up

MOVEMENT SERIES
- ❑ Sled Sprint—50 yards
- ❑ *L* Drill with Cones
- ❑ Lateral Single-Legged Ladders

CORE SERIES
- ❑ Pad Punches—20 reps each position

BLOCK 1 (FOUR CIRCUITS)
- ❑ Barbell High Pull/Clean/Front Squat—3 reps each side
- ❑ Rear Foot Elevated Barbell Split Squat—8 reps (first circuit), 6 reps (second), 4 reps (third), 3 reps (fourth)
- ❑ Sumo Squat to Hamstring Stretch—6 reps
- ❑ Jungle Gym (or TRX) Marches—10 reps

BLOCK 2 (THREE CIRCUITS)
- ❑ Contralateral Row—8 reps each side
- ❑ Stick Stretch—6 reps each side
- ❑ Lateral Box Jump—5 reps
- ❑ Medicine Ball Perpendicular Wall Throw—10 reps each side

BLOCK 3 (THREE CIRCUITS)
- ❑ Treadmill Push—30 seconds
- ❑ Dumbbell Wood Chop—8 reps each side
- ❑ Plank Sled Pull—25 yards

METABOLIC
- ❑ Battle Ropes—Three sets of 40 seconds

WEEK 10 – 235
MONDAY – 236
- ❑ Daily Warm-Up

MOVEMENT SERIES
- ❑ Position Specific

CORE SERIES
- ❑ Pillar Series—30 seconds each position

BLOCK 1 (FOUR CIRCUITS)
- ❑ Romanian Dead Lift to Power Shrug—8 reps
- ❑ Band Squat—10 reps (first circuit), 8 reps (second), 6 reps (third), 4 reps (fourth)
- ❑ Sumo Squat to Hamstring Stretch—6 reps
- ❑ Stability Ball Abs—15 Reps

BLOCK 2 (THREE CIRCUITS)
- ❑ Plate Row—12 reps

- ❑ Band RDL—8 reps
- ❑ Lateral Stretch—6 reps
- ❑ Plate Sit-Up to Rotation—8 reps each side

BLOCK 3 (THREE CIRCUITS)
- ❑ Band Thrusters—30 seconds
- ❑ Reactive Medicine Ball Wall Throw—5 reps each side
- ❑ Barbell Back Extension—10 reps
- ❑ Battle Ropes—30 seconds

METABOLIC
- ❑ Band Squat to Wrap—Three sets of 40 seconds

TUESDAY – 241
- ❑ Daily Warm-Up

MOVEMENT SERIES
- ❑ Position Specific

CORE SERIES
- ❑ Push-Up Scapular Pillar Series—30 seconds, 20 seconds each position

BLOCK 1 (FOUR CIRCUITS)
- ❑ Kettlebell Clean to Armpit—8 reps
- ❑ Kettlebell Squat to Press—12 reps (first circuit), 10 reps (second), 8 reps (third), 6 reps (fourth)
- ❑ Dumbbell Push-Up to Row—8 reps
- ❑ Heavy Weighted Abs—15 reps (start at 35 pounds and go up as needed)

BLOCK 2 (THREE CIRCUITS)
- ❑ Reverse Lunge with Plate Raise—5 reps each leg
- ❑ Plate Shrugs—25 reps
- ❑ Arnold Press—8 reps
- ❑ Three-Way Medicine Ball Push-Up—5 reps

BLOCK 3 (THREE CIRCUITS)
- ❑ Battle Rope Alternating Waves—20 reps each side
- ❑ Battle Rope Slams—20 reps
- ❑ Battle Rope Skiers—20 reps each side
- ❑ Triceps Kickback—30 seconds

METABOLIC
- ❑ Pull-Up Hold—3 reps at 40 seconds

WEDNESDAY – 245
- ❑ Daily Warm-Up
- ❑ Recovery

THURSDAY – 248
- ❑ Daily Warm-Up

MOVEMENT SERIES
- ❑ Position Specific

CORE SERIES
- [ ] Seated Medicine Ball Throws—Three sets of 20 reps

BLOCK 1 (FOUR CIRCUITS)
- [ ] Barbell High Pull/Clean/Press—3 reps each side
- [ ] Barbell Incline—10 reps (first circuit), 8 reps (second), 6 reps (third), 4 reps (fourth)
- [ ] Stability Ball Band Push-Up—10 reps
- [ ] Trigger Point—6 reps

BLOCK 2 (THREE CIRCUITS)
- [ ] Barbell Overhead Resistance Lunge—8 reps each leg
- [ ] Quad Hip Flexor Stretch—6 reps each side
- [ ] EGG Cradles—15 reps

BLOCK 3 (THREE CIRCUITS)
- [ ] Dead Ball Broad Jump—5 reps
- [ ] Wide-Legged Seated Kettlebell Rotational Press—8 reps
- [ ] Barbell Squat to Press—10 reps
- [ ] Jump Rope—2 minutes

METABOLIC
- [ ] Incline Band Flies—Three sets of 30 seconds

FRIDAY – 252
- [ ] Daily Warm-Up

MOVEMENT SERIES
- [ ] Position Specific

CORE SERIES
- [ ] Pad Punches—20 reps each position

BLOCK 1 (FOUR CIRCUITS)
- [ ] 3-Position Clean—3 reps
- [ ] Front Squat—10 reps (first circuit), 8 reps (second), 6 reps (third), 4 reps (fourth)
- [ ] Bike—30 seconds (first circuit), 45 seconds (second), 60 seconds (third), 75 seconds (fourth)
- [ ] Quad Hip Flexor Stretch—6 reps each side

BLOCK 2 (THREE CIRCUITS)
- [ ] Forward and Backward Lunge with Rotation—5 reps each side
- [ ] Neutral Pull-Up—10 reps
- [ ] Battle Rope Slams—30 reps
- [ ] Plate Holds—30 seconds

BLOCK 3 (THREE CIRCUITS)
- [ ] Incline Fly 1½—30 seconds
- [ ] Band Row 1½—30 seconds
- [ ] Tri Extension 1½—30 seconds
- [ ] Biceps Curl 1½—30 seconds

METABOLIC
- [ ] Treadmill—Three sets of 40 seconds

WEEK 11 – 257
MONDAY – 258
- [ ] Daily Warm-Up

MOVEMENT SERIES
- [ ] Position Specific

CORE SERIES
- [ ] Pillar Series—30 seconds each position

BLOCK 1 (FOUR CIRCUITS)
- [ ] Single-Arm Dumbbell Snatch to Press—4 reps each arm
- [ ] Incline Bench—10 reps (first circuit), 8 reps (second), 6 reps (third), 4 reps (fourth)
- [ ] Standing Ts—6 reps each leg
- [ ] Medicine Ball Chest Pass—30 seconds

BLOCK 2 (THREE CIRCUITS)
- [ ] Walking Lunge, Push-Up to Rotation—8 reps
- [ ] Kettlebell Eccentric Row—8 reps
- [ ] Dumbbell Push-Up to Row—8 reps
- [ ] Plate Sit-Ups—15 reps

BLOCK 3 (THREE CIRCUITS)
- [ ] Jungle Gym (or TRX) Stability Ball Push-Up—10 reps
- [ ] Lateral Hurdle to Push Sled—1 rep each side
- [ ] Medicine Ball Reverse Throw—5 reps
- [ ] Hips Elevated Alternate March—10 reps

METABOLIC
- [ ] Band High Pull—Three sets of 40 seconds

TUESDAY – 262
- [ ] Daily Warm-Up

MOVEMENT SERIES
- [ ] Position Specific

CORE SERIES
- [ ] Push-Up Scapular Pillar Series—30 seconds, 20 seconds each position

BLOCK 1 (FOUR CIRCUITS)
- [ ] Barbell High Pull, Snatch, Row, Forward Lunge—5 reps
- [ ] Barbell Step-Up—10 reps (first circuit), 8 reps (second), 6 reps (third), 4 reps (fourth)
- [ ] Quad Hip Flexor Stretch—6 reps each side
- [ ] Plate Sit-Ups—15 reps

BLOCK 2 (FOUR CIRCUITS)
- [ ] Dumbbell Bench Hips Off—5 reps
- [ ] Glute Activation—15 reps each side, then 15 with both legs together
- [ ] Box Jump Two to One—3 reps each side
- [ ] 90-Degree Pull-Up Hold—30 seconds

BLOCK 3 (FOUR CIRCUITS)
- [ ] Front Foot Elevated Lunge with Rotation—8 reps each leg
- [ ] Single-Legged Medicine Ball Slams—5 reps each leg
- [ ] Farmer's Walk—50 yards
- [ ] Kettlebell Sit-Up to Rotational Press—8 reps

METABOLIC
- [ ] Band Squat to Wrap—Three sets of 40 seconds

WEDNESDAY – 267
- [ ] Daily Warm-Up
- [ ] Recovery

THURSDAY – 268
- [ ] Daily Warm-Up

MOVEMENT SERIES
- [ ] Position Specific

CORE SERIES
- [ ] Seated Medicine Ball Throws—Three sets of 20 reps

BLOCK 1 (FOUR CIRCUITS)
- [ ] Barbell High Pull/Clean—4 reps
- [ ] Weighted Pull-Ups—8 reps (first circuit), 6 reps (second), 6 reps (third), 4 reps (fourth)
- [ ] Plate Front Raisers—10 reps
- [ ] Peanut—6 reps

BLOCK 2 (THREE CIRCUITS)
- [ ] Dead Ball Transverse Lateral Step-Up—8 reps each side
- [ ] Quad Hip Flexor Stretch—6 reps each side
- [ ] Sled Pull—25 yards
- [ ] Stability Ball Abs—30 seconds

BLOCK 3 (THREE CIRCUITS)
- [ ] Dumbbell Push-Up to Row—8 reps
- [ ] Split-Stance Medicine Ball Overhead Slams—5 reps each side
- [ ] Single-Legged Abdominal Sliders—15 reps each leg

METABOLIC
- [ ] Tire Flips—Three sets of 40 seconds

FRIDAY – 272

❏ Daily Warm-Up

MOVEMENT SERIES
❏ Position Specific

CORE SERIES
❏ Pad Punches—20 reps each position

BLOCK 1 (FOUR CIRCUITS)
❏ Band Squat—30 seconds
❏ Bike—30 seconds
❏ Speed Barbell Band Bench—30 seconds
❏ Kettlebell Ballistic Row—30 seconds

BLOCK 2 (THREE CIRCUITS)
❏ Battle Ropes—30 seconds
❏ Triceps Kickback—30 seconds
❏ Band Bi (Bicep Curls with Band)—30 seconds

BLOCK 3 (THREE CIRCUITS)
❏ Plank Ball Roll—30 seconds each direction
❏ 90-Degree Pull-Up Hold—30 seconds

METABOLIC
❏ Bench—Three sets of 40 seconds

WEEK 12 – 277
MONDAY – 278

❏ Daily Warm-Up

MOVEMENT SERIES
❏ Position Specific

CORE SERIES
❏ Pillar Series—30 seconds each position

BLOCK 1 (FOUR CIRCUITS)
❏ Snatch Grip High Pull—8 reps
❏ Barbell Bench—10 reps (first circuit), 8 reps (second), 6 reps (third), 4 reps (fourth)
❏ Plate Front Raisers—10 reps
❏ Ab Rollout—15 reps

BLOCK 2 (THREE CIRCUITS)
❏ Ipsilateral Kettlebell Step-Up to Press—5 reps each side
❏ Band RDL—8 reps
❏ Bent Knee Hamstring Stretch—6 reps each leg
❏ Dead Ball Wall Throw—5 reps

BLOCK 3 (THREE CIRCUITS)
❏ Kettlebell Neutral Lunge—5 reps
❏ Dumbbell Hammer Curl—10 reps

❏ Front Foot Elevated Split-Stance Medicine Ball Toss—10 reps each side
❏ 90-Degree Pull-Up Hold—30 seconds

METABOLIC
❏ Battle Ropes—Three sets of 40 seconds

TUESDAY – 282

❏ Daily Warm-Up

MOVEMENT SERIES
❏ Position Specific

CORE SERIES
❏ Push-Up Scapular Pillar Series—20 seconds, 10 seconds each position

BLOCK 1 (FOUR CIRCUITS)
❏ Resistance Kettlebell Swing—15 reps
❏ Walking Lunge with Rotation—10 reps (first circuit), 8 reps (second), 6 reps (third), 4 reps (fourth)
❏ Push-Pull Sled—25 yards
❏ Jungle Gym/TRX Body Saw—15 reps

BLOCK 2 (THREE CIRCUITS)
❏ Horizontal Row—12 reps
❏ Kettlebell Reverse Fly—15 reps
❏ Battle Ropes—30 seconds

BLOCK 3 (THREE CIRCUITS)
❏ Heavy Dumbbell Bench—5 reps
❏ Medicine Ball Perpendicular Wall Throw—5 reps each side
❏ Lateral Step-Up with Plate Extension—8 reps each side
❏ Glute Bridge—30 seconds

METABOLIC
❏ Lateral Pull Down—Three sets of 40 seconds

WEDNESDAY – 288

❏ Daily Warm-Up
❏ Recovery

THURSDAY – 287

❏ Daily Warm-Up

MOVEMENT SERIES
❏ Position Specific

CORE SERIES
❏ Seated Medicine Ball Throws—Three sets of 20 reps

BLOCK 1 (FOUR CIRCUITS)
❏ Three Position High Pull—3 reps
❏ Incline Dumbbell Bench Press (135 pounds)—10 reps
❏ Medicine Ball Chest Pass—30 seconds
❏ Stick Stretch—6 reps each side

BLOCK 2 (THREE CIRCUITS)
❏ Barbell Single-Legged Hip Thrust—5 reps each side
❏ Sumo Squat to Hamstring Stretch—6 reps
❏ Band Jump with Medicine Ball—5 reps
❏ Dumbbell Side Bends—15 reps each side

BLOCK 3 (THREE CIRCUITS)
❏ Base Position Twist with Extension—10 reps each side
❏ Tripod Push-Ups—30 seconds
❏ Heavy Weighted Abs—15 reps (start at 35 pounds and go up as needed)
❏ Skull Crushers—12 reps

METABOLIC
❏ Triceps Extension—Three sets of 40 seconds

FRIDAY – 291

❏ Daily Warm-Up

MOVEMENT SERIES
❏ Position Specific

CORE SERIES
❏ Pad Punches—20 reps each position

BLOCK 1 (FOUR CIRCUITS)
❏ Barbell High Pull, Snatch, Row, Forward Lunge—5 reps
❏ Weighted Pull-Ups—10 reps
❏ Dumbbell Push-Up to Row—8 reps
❏ Plate Shrugs—30 seconds

BLOCK 2 (THREE CIRCUITS)
❏ Valslide Lateral Lunge with Extension—8 reps each side
❏ Kettlebell Push/Pull—10 reps each side
❏ Heavy Pull Sled—25 yards
❏ Weighted Plank—30 seconds

BLOCK 3 (THREE CIRCUITS)
❏ Single-Legged Squat—8 reps each leg
❏ Back Foot Elevated Dead Ball Rotational Chop—10 reps each side
❏ Battle Ropes—30 seconds
❏ 90-Degree Pull-Up Hold—30 seconds

METABOLIC
❏ Supine Biceps—Three sets of 40 seconds

ACKNOWLEDGMENTS

I want to thank my family for their continued support: Chrissy, Moms, Pops, Sis, Arian, Furman, Brax, Glass and Red. My guys Dose and Leo for being the backbone of the training culture we are attempting to push. All of the clients/ brothers that have given us an opportunity to aid in the betterment of their careers. To Kara for all of your efforts in helping us to make this program possible. To the great people at Page Street Publishing for giving a kid with a dream a chance. And to all of the aspiring athletes, you all are our motivation! Train hard!

ABOUT THE AUTHOR

Abdul Foster is a professional trainer, fitness coach and counselor to many of the top players in the NFL. He is known for his elite training style. Abdul himself is an elite athlete, a former track star and a competitor at heart, so he understands his clients and always wants them to excel. Through his extensive training sessions, he ensures that not only are his clients' bodies at their best, but their minds are prepared for the challenges of professional football as well.

Growing up in Albuquerque, New Mexico, Abdul brought home nearly 20 awards during his high school years, including two state titles in track and field hurdles. He still holds the state record for the 110-meter hurdles. He went on to star on the track and field team at Florida A&M University. With his own elite athletic background, he truly understands the necessary hard work.

In 2009, he created Elite Life Training and traveled across the country training some of the top athletes in sports. He opened Nine Innovations in Houston in 2014, taking his lifelong love of sports and turning it into more than just a business about personal training. Abdul doesn't just provide the drills, he does the behind-the-scenes work necessary—from nutrition to sports medicine—to ensure that any athlete he works with will be at their best. He knows his athletes inside and out. He knows what the physical requirements are on the field and what's needed off the field as well.

As a trainer, Abdul has trained some of the NFL's top athletes who went to the Pro Bowl, including wide receiver Andre Johnson, offensive lineman Duane Brown, tight end Owen Daniels and safety Glover Quin.

In his time as a trainer, Abdul has been a part of several remarkable success stories, including that of his younger brother, running back Arian Foster. Abdul has trained Arian since college, helping him through his transition to the NFL. Arian only made the practice squad with the Texans, but Abdul was determined to do what was necessary to help Arian make the roster. With a unique and intensive training routine, designed specifically for Arian's body and needs for his position, he made the team and had an explosive year in 2010, breaking several franchise and NFL records.

Abdul earned his National Academy of Sports Medicine certification and has pursued a business degree. He has been credited by many athletes for being more than a trainer, but a counselor who cares and takes on their goals as his own.

With the Nine Innovations training program, Abdul takes his understanding of what it takes to be the best and translates it into something that is more than just a business—it's a new breed of training.

INDEX